THE ALL OCCASION
CHICKEN
COOKBOOK

MURDOCH BOOKS®
Sydney • London • Vancouver • New York

CONTENTS

All About Chicken

CHOOSING AND BUYING

Today you can buy chicken in almost any shape or form — fresh, chilled, frozen, whole, or in joints (pieces) or fillets. Most shopping centres have at least one fresh chicken shop which sells whole chickens, chicken pieces, marinated chicken joints and kebabs and cooked barbecued chicken. Cooked chicken is also widely available from major chains or drive-in takeaways and enterprising smaller shops, which is a helpful short-cut in providing family meals.

Lean chicken cuts are an excellent choice for the health conscious. Chicken is a valuable protein food, it also contains B group vitamins as well as minerals and is very easy to digest.

Prime consideration when you are making a selection of a whole bird for cooking is the size and age of the bird as this dictates your cooking method. Sizes are coded as numbers on the packaging. When you realise that a No 12 chicken weighs 1.2 kg, a No 14 chicken weighs 1.4 kg, a No 16 chicken weighs 1.6 kg and so on, the problem of what size to buy is demystified. A No 15 chicken, that is one that weighs 1.5 kg is a good size to serve 4 people.

Young chickens, poussin, spatchcock and capons are tender, delicately flavoured and well suited to roasting, grilling or barbecuing. Chickens ranging from No 12 to No 16 are ideal for roasting. When buying fresh chicken, look for plumpness of the breast and smooth unblemished skin.

Larger, mature birds generally have tougher meat — particularly on their thighs — and are best cooked slowly to prevent them drying out. These 'boiler' birds retain their succulence and flavour if gently braised or poached with vegetables and herbs. If you choose not to use all the liquid in which the chicken is cooked, it can be saved and used as a flavoursome stock, invaluable in making soups, sautées, stir-frys and casseroles.

The best guide to a bird's age, apart from obvious indications like size, is the flexibility of its frame — test this by pressing the breast bone; if it bends, then the chicken is young and suitable for all of the speedy cooking methods.

We often buy chicken pieces today, as it is more versatile and convenient, quick to cook and some cuts are more economical than buying a whole bird. Select small-boned but plump jointed pieces and succulent fillets rather than large but potentially dry and stringy portions. The chicken should not be slimy or have an 'off' smell. Shop at a fresh chicken shop which has a regular turnover for good quality fresh chicken.

SIZE GUIDE FOR CHICKEN AND POULTRY

Chicken

BOILING FOWL: 1.8 kg to 3 kg are best suited to slow cooking methods with plenty of liquid to prevent them drying out.

ROASTING BIRDS: 1.2 kg to 1.6 kg are the ideal weight for tender roast chicken, serving 4 to 6 people but chickens weighing up to 2 kg can be succulent and tender.

CAPONS: Castrated young cockerels which have been specially fattened. They weigh between 3.6 kg to 4.6 kg and their fleshy frames give good value for a Christmas dinner.

SPRING CHICKEN: An excellent option for a couple as these small birds weigh in at 900 g to 1.1 kg and provide enough to feed two comfortably.

POUSSIN OR SPATCHCOCK: These are baby chickens which weigh 350 g to 450 g. Larger birds may stretch to two people but smaller birds make an ample single serving and are extremely succulent.

CHICKEN PIECES: 500 g boneless chicken, such as breast and/or thigh fillets serves 4 people; 1 kg chicken pieces on the bone serves 4 people. Boneless chicken pieces cook quicker than chicken pieces on the bone.

Poultry

QUAIL: These are tiny birds which are generally sold in pairs and more often served as an entrée than a main course as they have very little meat but a delicate and distinctive flavour.

PIGEON: Though older birds are best braised, pot roasted or made into a pie, young pigeons can be very tastily roasted or grilled. Depending on size, they will serve 1 to 2 people.

GUINEA FOWL: You will get as much meat off guinea fowl as a medium-sized chicken, and it has a slightly gamey taste.

PHEASANT: One bird will usually serve two people and, because of the meat's tendency to dry out, it is well suited to gentle braising as well as to more traditional roasting.

TURKEY: These birds are extremely variable in size — they're sold at weights anywhere between 2.6 kg and 14 kg. You should allow 275 g to 350 g per serving. Slow roasting is preferable, after the bird starts to sizzle.

GOOSE: This rich and rather fatty bird usually weighs between 2.6 kg to 6.3 kg and makes a particularly popular festive dish often complemented by fruit and vegetable stuffings to balance the flavour of the strong-tasting flesh. Allow 350 g to 400 g per serving.

DUCK: Though duck should generally be eaten young rather than fully grown, it should weigh no less than 1.4 kg or there's too much bone and too little meat. You should allow 450 g dressed weight per serving.

PREPARATION

You can serve chicken in many different ways — whole, jointed, boned or filleted — oven roasted, spit roasted, barbecued, grilled, sautéed, stir-fried, casseroled.

Poultry should be cooked very fresh — within a day or two of killing, unless it has been frozen. With game, it's a different story. To improve the flavour and tenderise the meat, the birds may be hung for up to a fortnight.

Young chicken and duckling as well as goose have enough fat under the skin to roast successfully without drying out, but many game birds are too lean to be placed in a hot oven and cooked. They need a protective covering called 'barding' to prevent them drying and toughening. This can be done with either a layer of pork fat or other fat or bacon.

Before they are roasted, chickens should be wiped over with a damp cloth and then patted dry; the birds will not brown effectively if they are put into the oven wet. It's a good idea to truss poultry as this keeps the bird in shape and also prevents leakage of any stuffing placed in the body cavity. Strings used to truss the bird should be removed before carving.

Stuffing serves more than one purpose; apart from enhancing the flavour of the meat with its more aromatic ingredients, it makes a tasty accompaniment to the meal, sometimes in place of a rich sauce. Additionally, it helps provide a boned bird with substance and shape.

While poultry should, as a rule, be very thoroughly cooked, dark-fleshed game birds are often served underdone or even rare for best results. However so long as you take steps to prevent the meat drying out (such as using foil) there's nothing to stop you cooking these birds until they're past the slightly pink stage, if that's the way you prefer them.

STEP-BY-STEP PREPARATION TECHNIQUES

Jointing a Chicken

STEP 1   With the chicken on its back, cut between the thigh and body of chicken through the hip joint. Bend the leg back and the hip joint will be easily found. Cut through hip joint, remove leg. Repeat with other leg.

STEP 2   Place leg skin side down. Cut through thigh joint.

STEP 3   Turn chicken on its side. Pull wing away from body and cut through wing joint. Repeat with remaining wing.

STEP 4   Working from the tail end towards the neck cut through the bones connecting breast to the backbone and along the collarbone.

STEP 5   Turn chicken over and repeat with the other side. Chicken will be hinged by collarbone. Pull backbone away from breast and discard.

STEP 6   With chicken breast skin side up, cut lengthwise into two along the breastbone. Breast may be cut across to form four pieces if desired.

Boning a Chicken

STEP 1   Turn the bird on its breast, tail end furthest away. Slice the flesh cleanly down the backbone towards the tail, carefully filleting the meat by cutting against the bone so as not to pierce the skin. Hold the flesh close to the carcass to prevent tearing. Gradually ease the meat away until you reach the wing and thigh joints; loosen flesh around these, then pause.

STEP 2   Place knife between the cartilage knuckles of both the wings and thighs and they should break away without sawing through the bone.

STEP 3   Loosen the breast meat away by gently scraping the knife against the ribs. Pull the ribcage away and remove any white cartilage still adhering to the central breast. Cut off the tail and the bird should be lying flat.

STEP 4   Slice off the end section of the wings, then cut into the flesh around the joint to release the tendons and gently work the meat off the bone. Push the meat from the boned wings into the body of the bird.

STEP 5   Cut around the bottom end of each leg to release the tendons and scrape the knife up the bone to where the drumstick meat begins. Twist the bone so that it comes away at the socket and do the same with the other leg. Remove any stray pieces of cartilage from the now boned chicken and scrape off any meat still remaining on the carcass and push it into the rest of the flesh, which is ready to be stuffed.

NOTE: *A good butcher will often do this for you but you may have to pay for his time!*

Boning a Drumstick

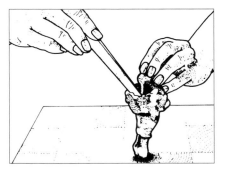

STEP 1   Cut around leg joint with a sharp knife to sever all tendons and sinew, making it easier to separate flesh from bone.

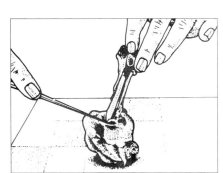

STEP 2   Peel flesh down and away from the bone. When you reach the next knuckle, cut through tendons and sinew so that the flesh is completely loosened from the bone.

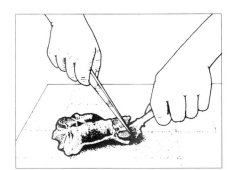

STEP 3   Peel flesh inside out exposing the bone. Cut through the bone at the base leaving the knuckle attached to the flesh. This acts as a base and keeps stuffing inside the leg. Turn flesh so skin is on the outside.

Deboning a Chicken Breast

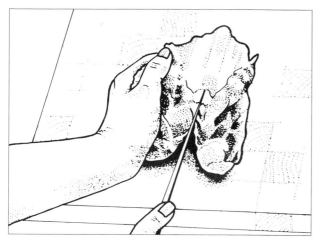

STEP 1   Place breast skin side down on work surface. Cut a small slit into the cartilage and skin at the widest end of the breast.

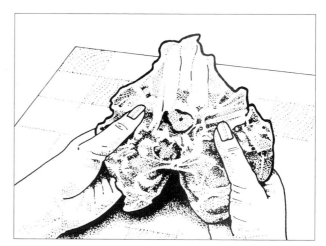

STEP 2   Bend the breast backwards to snap the breastbone.

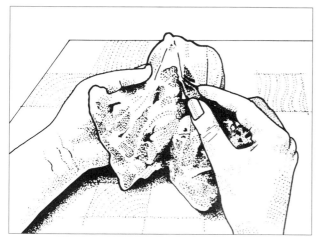

STEP 3   With the fingers loosen the flesh away from the large white keel bone. Pull keel bone upwards and discard.

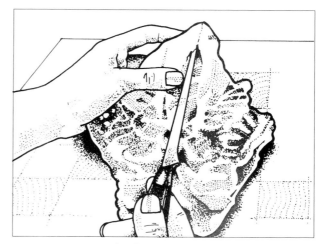

STEP 4   Using a knife remove cartilage from breast.

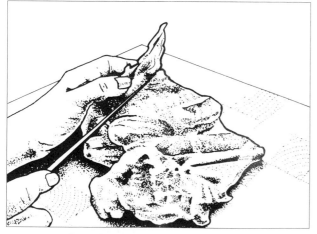

STEP 5   Slip a knife under rib bones and scrape away the meat. Remove the tiny bones.

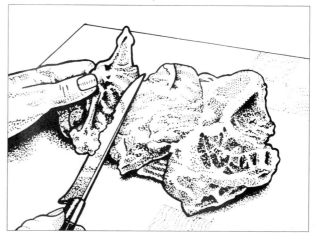

STEP 6   Cut meat away from collarbones. Remove bone then proceed with the other side of the breast.

Trussing

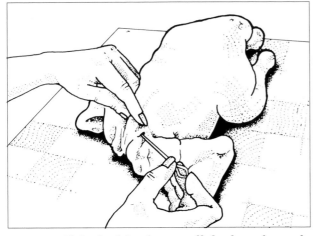

STEP 1   If the bird has been stuffed, close the neck end by folding the skin flap over the bird's back and secure with a skewer.

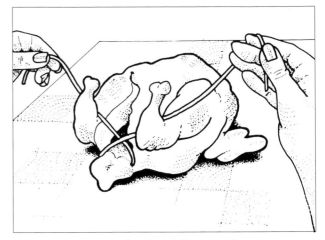

STEP 2   Place the bird with leg tips facing upwards. Take a long length of string, encircle the parson's nose, bring the string up and over the legs.

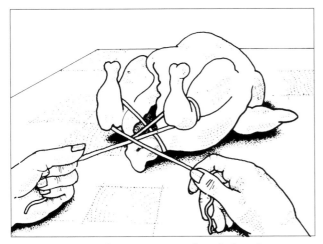

STEP 3   Loop the string around each leg then cross the string above the parson's nose. Turn bird over.

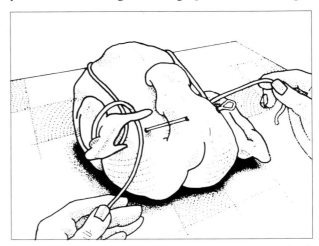

STEP 4   Bring the string along the sides of the bird and wrap around the wings.

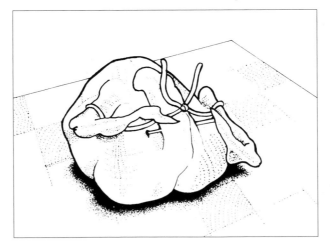

STEP 5   Bring both ends of the string to the centre, gently pull so that the wings compact to form a neat shape, then secure the string in a knot.

Carving a Chicken

You'll need a sharp, pointed knife with a long flexible blade plus a long two-pronged fork with a raised guard to hold the bird securely while you carve it.

STEP 1   Place the bird on a carving dish, breast side up, and hold it in place with a carving fork. Cut through the joint where the leg is attached to the carcass. Lift the leg away and divide into two portions cutting through the joint where the drumstick meets the thigh.

STEP 2   Carve down through the breast and sever the wing through the joint. Remove with a portion of the breast.

STEP 3   With the bird on its side carve through the wishbone (at the neck end of breast) and remove with some of the meat.

STEP 4   Turn the bird so that the neck end is facing you and carve thin slices from the breast.

STEP 5   Turn the carcass breast side down and remove the oyster fillets situated either side of the backbone.

STORAGE

Storing and Freezing

Obviously all poultry should be kept refrigerated, as meat deteriorates quickly, especially in warmer climates. It's important to remove the giblets from inside the bird as quickly as possible as they give the meat an unpalatable, bitter taste. Giblets should also be cooked promptly, as they have a shorter life than the flesh of the bird. They should also be stored separately.

Poultry can be safely refrigerated in the coldest section of the fridge for up to three days, though you should be cautious about even this timescale if the weather is exceptionally hot. For best results, you should remove the bird from any wrapping, wash thoroughly, dry with a paper towel, and cover it loosely with plastic wrapping that lets air circulate.

With freezing, the technique is slightly different. If you've bought a ready-frozen bird, then obviously you cannot thaw it to remove the giblets and then refreeze the meat without cooking it. If you've bought fresh poultry, then it's wise to remove the giblets and cook or store them separately from the main bird. You should cover the meat tightly with foil or put it in a polythene freezer bag and seal it tightly, making sure that you squeeze out or suck out with a straw as much air as possible. Fresh chicken will freeze successfully for 4 to 6 months, duck and goose 4 to 5 months and turkey 6 months.

Thawing

For safety's sake, it's vital that you stick to the rules when thawing poultry; every bit of the bird should be thawed before you cook it and failure to do this could result in a nasty case of food poisoning. Once the meat has started to thaw, you cannot refreeze it; this encourages bacterial growth and with that the risk of poisoning. For the same reason, a thawed bird should be cooked as soon as possible, particularly in warm climates, where meat goes bad quickly. Poultry must be thawed gradually in the refrigerator as it can go off fast if allowed to defrost at room temperature. Additionally, the bird will lose less of its moisture and succulence in the fridge.

If the process takes longer than you anticipated, you can take some cautious steps to speed up the thawing; it does no harm to pull the wings and thighs away from the body, remove the defrosting giblets from inside, and gently open the cavity to allow air to circulate. More radically you can hold the bird under the cold running tap, particularly if almost all but the internal section is ice-free. The simplest method of thawing is to microwave the poultry, but do this according to the oven manufacturer's own instructions.

Average thawing times in the refrigerator are:

1 kg — 13 hours
1.5 kg — 15 hours
2 kg — 17 hours
2.5 kg — 20 hours
3 kg — 24 hours
3.5 kg — 28 hours.

COOKING METHODS

ROASTING: This technique is suitable only for young birds as the intense heat which cooks the meat tends to have a drying and toughening effect on older poultry. In roasting, the skin and underlying fat cook rapidly and in doing so form a seal around the bird and allow its own juices to spread inward and cook the flesh more gently.

GRILLING/BARBECUING: This is when radiant, or conducted heat is applied to only one side of the meat at a time. Again it is best suited to young tender birds — spatchcocks sliced in half and laid flat, or breast fillets or joints. Leave the skin on during cooking unless marinated as this prevents the natural juices escaping and drying the meat out. To moisten it further, the chicken should be basted throughout the cooking process with either oil, butter or marinade. Barbecuing works the same way and the total cooking

time for either method is around 40 minutes for joints or halved spatchcocks, but as little as 15 minutes for breast fillets.

ROTISSERIE: This combines the virtues of both roasting and grilling, with the meat both seared and cooked by all round heat as it turns on a spit. Again, it produces best results when tender young birds are used.

PAN-FRYING: Here, direct heat is applied to the meat via the pan, searing the flesh and sealing in the juices. At this point the temperature should be reduced so the chicken can cook more gently until tender. Small joints or breast fillets are best and they should be turned frequently to prevent burning. It also makes sense to use a non-stick frying pan as this reduces the need for added oil to moisten the meat. Chicken strips and cubes are often fried before adding to pasta or rice dishes.

SAUTÉING: This combines pan-frying and poaching or simmering. A sauté pan or a large frying pan may be used. Boneless chicken joints/pieces are ideal. They should be sealed first then liquid is added keeping the chicken meat moist while it completes cooking by simmering gently.

STIR-FRYING: Traditional Chinese cooking is very popular. It's very similar to pan-frying, except that a round-bottomed 'wok' is used, the meat is cut into fine strips and stirred round rapidly in a dash of hot oil and whatever seasonings and vegetables are needed for fast and succulent serving. This is the most healthy method of frying as it

requires so little fat and the fast cooking method preserves the maximum quantity of nutritious juices.

CASSEROLING: An ideal way of getting best results from an older, rather tough bird. By immersing the whole bird or jointed chicken pieces into water seasoned with herbs, spices, vegetables and/or pulses, the meat loses none of its succulence and becomes flavoursome and tender in the liquid. Casseroles can be cooked in the oven, on a hot plate in a special cast iron pan or in a special slow cooker which will ensure that none of the liquid simmers away.

DEEP-FRYING: This requires a deep pan and plenty of oil heated to a high temperature so that the meat is seared and sealed as soon as it is placed in the fat. Coating the chicken pieces in seasoned flour, egg and breadcrumbs forms a crust around the meat that prevents the escape of flavoursome and nutritious juices, but at the same time reduces the quantity of fat absorbed into the flesh during cooking. Large portions of meat are unsuited to this method. It is used for traditional Chicken Maryland but is not recommended as a regular healthy cooking method.

MICROWAVING: By placing a whole or jointed chicken into a microwave oven, you can cook many of the dishes you prepare with traditional methods in just a fraction of the time. Whole chickens can be roasted, but small portions and joints are particularly suited to microwaving as they cook very evenly.

TECHNIQUES WITH STUFFING AND STOCK

Stuffing

This seems to go hand in hand with chicken and other fowl. There are recipes created to complement all types of poultry and game. Stuffing is particularly important for boned birds as it gives them shape and turns them into exotic dishes. Not all such fillings are meant to be eaten. Tiny game birds, for instance, absorb a lot of flavour from strong but discardable stuffings like clove-studded onions or juniper berries while larger and rather fatty birds are improved with stuffings that will add tang to the flesh, but can be thrown out when they absorb fat and juices from the meat.

Cardinal rules to remember are that extra cooking time must be allowed for stuffed birds, and that it's important not to over-stuff the body cavity as the filling expands and overflows during the cooking process and will push its way out of the bird and be spoiled or wasted.

Stock

Many of us automatically turn to ready-made stock cubes and powders when we need a seasoned stock, rather than taking the simple steps to make our own. While cubes and powders have a convenient role in modern cookery, they are high in salt and far less nutritious than a stock made from chicken bones, vegetables, herbs and spices. Additionally, they do not provide the subtle flavouring of a home-made stock. A stock will provide the basis for soup, sauces and casseroles and can be kept for up to 6 months in the freezer. If you're short on storage space it can be reduced to a concentrate by boiling until most of the liquid evaporates, then frozen in ice cube trays so you have as little or as much as required for your recipes. Stock is not a dish in itself but makes the basis of many tasty chicken dishes. See page 28 for a traditional stock recipe.

HANDY HINTS

- 1.5 kg roast/barbecued chicken yields 4 cups cooked chicken meat.
- Always allow your chicken to 'rest' for a few minutes before carving — it makes the job far easier.
- Before freezing, make sure your meat or stock cools down as fast as possible (reducing the risk of bacterial growth) by putting it into pre-chilled containers.
- Use non-stick pans where possible as it cuts down on the need for fat

in your chicken dishes.

• Remove the giblets as soon as possible from your poultry as this will prevent the flesh acquiring a bitter tang.

• Prepare stuffing in advance if you wish, but remember never to put it inside the bird until you're ready to cook it — it will sour the flavour of the meat.

• If you're cooking for a crowd, remember that smaller joints of poultry will go further than large ones.

• Most of the fat on fowl is stored immediately under the skin, so remove this where possible, and cook the meat skinless.

• The white meat of poultry contains the least fat and the dark meat the most fat.

• When cooking game, remember it has a tendency to dry out so, unless the bird is particularly fatty, bard it by criss-crossing it with pork fat over the top or coating it with butter or bacon.

• Never attempt to speed up the thawing process by soaking fowl in hot water or running it under the hot tap — this could encourage the growth of bacteria.

• Before cooking game, singe off any stubborn feathers or quills by holding the bird over a low gas flame and turning it slowly, or by moving a lighted candle around the body.

• While the oil glands of most birds are quite harmless, in the case of duck they give the flesh a musky taste and should be cut out with a sharp knife before cooking.

• Try stuffing fowl under the skin, rather than in the body cavity. It

can only be done with a fresh bird and it's important not to tear the skin when pulling it away from the flesh, so pinch it all over first.

• Microwave small rather than large portions of poultry as these will cook and brown more uniformly.

• Before roasting duck or goose, prick the skin all over to release fat for basting during the cooking process.

• Chicken is lower in fat (and therefore in kilojoules) than practically all meats and many fowl, so makes a good addition to a weight reducing diet.

• Commercially frozen and wrapped chicken will keep for as much as twice the time — say 12 months — as home frozen birds.

• Use cheaper cuts of chicken to pad out large-scale dishes — remember that thighs and wings are lower in cost than the white meat and, on average, than a whole bird, so use them to supplement whole joints when entertaining large numbers.

• Never put turnips or parsnips into a stock as they will cloud the liquid.

USEFUL EQUIPMENT FOR COOKING POULTRY

BAKING DISH: Also called a roasting tin. It's worth investing in a dish with a rack that will elevate your bird, so fat can run off in the cooking process.

BASTING BULB: Use one of these to pour oil or marinade over the cooking bird and you'll save mess, as well as the risk of burned hands with a spoon.

BONING KNIFE: Sharpness and manoeuvrability are the features to look for.

CARVING FORK: A safety requirement in that, if the knife slips while you are carving, its guard will save you from cuts. A large fork is also more effective in securing the bird.

FOIL: Strong aluminium foil is invaluable when roasting poultry, as a seal to keep the juices in. It also keeps chilled dishes in good shape. Choose a brand that's either fairly tough or has a strong bursting strength — there's nothing so annoying as foil that tears every time you try to stretch it or wrap it round sharp bones.

TRUSSING NEEDLE AND COTTON: Important for trussing poultry. You'll need a special large needle for the job and strong cotton to hold the bird securely.

PASTRY BRUSH: Useful for glazing chicken and can also be used to brush cooking meat with butter or juices.

POULTRY SCISSORS OR SHEARS: Strong poultry scissors are a great aid to jointing the bird and snapping through bones.

SKEWERS (METAL AND BAMBOO): Important for holding the flesh together and vital, of course, when making kebabs. Bamboo looks nicer, but metal has an unlimited life.

STRING: Use strong cotton string for trussing your fowl.

Equipment for cooking chicken. From bottom right clockwise: kitchen string, small metal skewers, aluminium foil, poultry shears, trussing needle, boning knife, pastry brush.

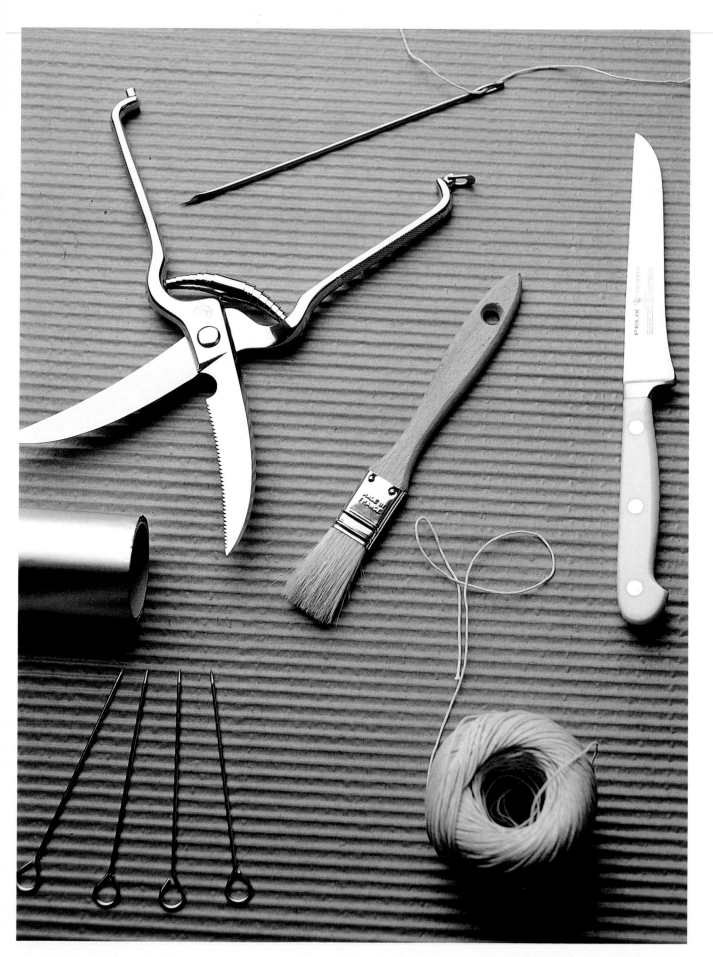

Finger Licking Chicken

*F*inger food recipes for parties and picnics, snacks and starters, sandwiches and packed lunches are in this section.

The recipes are versatile and offer hints for preparing the food in advance — a must for finger licking party snacks.

CHICKEN AND TOMATO MELTS

8 slices buttered wholegrain toast

8 slices cooked chicken

8 slices large tomato

125 g (4 oz) grated tasty cheese

2 teaspoons Worcestershire sauce

herbs or salad greens for serving

Arrange toast in shallow baking dish. Place a slice of chicken on each piece and top with a slice of tomato. Mix cheese with sauce and spread thickly over top. Brown under hot grill until cheese has melted.

Serve hot garnished with fresh herbs or salad greens for a nourishing snack.

SERVES 8

Dishes on previous pages: Chicken Burghul Balls (page 16), Focaccia with Chicken and Sun Dried Tomatoes (page 24), Chicken Sate with Peanut Sauce (page 17)

CHICKEN BURGHUL BALLS

These are popular with children for a picnic or packed lunch; also a good finger-licking party savoury.

30 g (1 oz) burghul

500 g (1 lb) chicken mince

2 thinly sliced spring onions (shallots)

4 sprigs of continental parsley, chopped

grated rind of 1 lemon

60 g (2 oz) grated cheddar cheese

1 egg, beaten

¼ teaspoon white pepper

sesame seeds and extra burghul for coating

olive oil for frying

Soak burghul in 1 cup (250 ml/ 8 fl oz) cold water for 30 minutes. Drain well and squeeze dry with the fingertips. Mix burghul with chicken

Chicken and Tomato Melts

mince, spring onion, parsley, lemon rind, cheese, egg and pepper.

Shape into 24 small balls with clean wet hands. Roll balls in an equal mixture of sesame seeds and burghul until coated.

Heat sufficient oil to cover the bottom of a large heavy frying pan and gently fry chicken balls until golden brown on all sides and cooked through in centre. Serve warm or cold with a tzadziki dipping sauce (see page 55) or pack for a picnic.

MAKES APPROXIMATELY 24

CHICKEN SATE WITH PEANUT SAUCE

This is delicious finger licking party food and may also be served as an entrée at an Asian dinner party.

2 large chicken breast fillets

1 onion, finely chopped

75 g (2½ oz) ground peanuts

2 cloves garlic, crushed

1 teaspoon minced chilli

pinch of salt

juice of 2 limes

PEANUT SAUCE

½ cup (125 ml/4 fl oz) crunchy peanut butter

½ cup (125 ml/4 fl oz) coconut milk

2 tablespoons light soy sauce

juice of ½ lemon

2 cloves garlic, crushed

1 teaspoon minced chilli

1 teaspoon honey, optional

Cut chicken into 2.5 cm (1 in) cubes. Mix remaining ingredients together in a food processor or blender. Add mixture to chicken, stir well until coated then cover and marinate in refrigerator for at least 1 hour.

Thread chicken onto 8 pre-soaked bamboo skewers. Cook under a medium–hot grill, turning frequently and brushing with remaining marinade, for 5 to 6 minutes until cooked.

Peanut Sauce: Mix all ingredients together and heat through gently.

Serve chicken saté with warm peanut sauce for dipping or spooning over.

**SERVES 8,
SERVES 4 FOR AN ENTRÉE**

MINI SPRING ROLLS

2 chicken breast fillets, skinned

1 onion

90 g (3 oz) mushrooms

2 carrots

¼ head Chinese cabbage

4 tablespoons oil

30 g (1 oz) bean sprouts

3 tablespoons soy sauce

salt and pepper

2 eggs

*50 mini spring roll wrappers
(12.5 x 12.5 cm/5 x 5 in)*

oil for deep frying

Mince chicken and onion in food processor or electric blender. Then mince mushrooms, carrots and cabbage in food processor. Heat oil in a frying pan, add chicken mixture and cook for 3 minutes. Add vegetables, including bean sprouts, cook for 4 minutes, stirring constantly. Add soy sauce and season to taste. Cool slightly and stir in 1 egg.

Place 2 heaped teaspoonfuls of mixture on each wrapper. Make 5 at a time while keeping remainder covered with damp cloth. Beat other egg and brush edges of wrappers. Roll up securely (see photograph).

Deep-fry rolls in hot oil until golden brown. Serve with a bowl of soy sauce for dipping.

Serve hot as a party savoury, or for a first course of an Asian meal.

Note: Rolls can be made in advance and frozen until ready for use. Partly thaw before frying.

MAKES 50

Cook minced mixture in frying pan. Add soy sauce, stir constantly.

Place filling on spring roll wrapper, brush edges with beaten egg and roll up. Keep remaining wrappers covered with damp cloth.

Deep-fry in hot oil until golden brown.

CRUNCHY CHICKEN LIVERS WITH SOUR CREAM DIP

50 g (1⅔ oz) cornmeal

30 g (1 oz) plain (all-purpose) flour, sifted

½ teaspoon garlic salt

pinch pepper

1 egg, beaten

2 tablespoons milk

7 chicken livers

oil for deep frying

SOUR CREAM DIP

1 cup (250 ml/8 fl oz) sour cream

2 tablespoons finely grated onion

¼ teaspoon salt

1 teaspoon French wholegrain mustard

4 drops Tabasco or chilli sauce

To make livers: Clean livers, remove membrane and cut into lobes. Combine cornmeal, flour and seasonings. Mix egg with the milk. Dip each piece of liver into the seasoned cornmeal, then into egg mixture and then into cornmeal again.

Heat sufficient oil in a small, straight-sided pan to come half way up the sides.

Deep-fry chicken livers at 190°C (375°F) for 2 minutes or until golden brown. Drain well on kitchen paper towels. Serve warm on cocktail sticks with dip.

To make dip: Combine all ingredients, cover and refrigerate until ready to serve.

Serve Crunchy Chicken Livers and dip accompanied by crudités (small pieces of fresh vegetables) for a party savoury.

Crunchy Chicken Livers with Sour Cream Dip

Note: These appetisers can be prepared in advance. To reheat livers place in a 180°C (350°F) oven for about 10 minutes.

MAKES ABOUT 30 PLUS 1 CUP OF DIP

HAM AND CHICKEN PIN WHEELS

4 chicken breast fillets, skinned

pinch dried basil

salt

freshly ground pepper

4 thin slices cooked ham or prosciutto

1 clove garlic, crushed

2 tablespoons fresh lemon juice

paprika

24 toasted or fried bread rounds (croûts)

Preheat oven to 180°C (350°F).

Put chicken, top side down, on board between two sheets of clear plastic wrap or greaseproof paper, pound to 5 mm (¼ in) thickness with a rolling pin or meat mallet. Sprinkle with basil, salt and pepper. Cover each breast with 1 slice ham. Roll lengthwise with ham inside, and secure with toothpicks.

Arrange, seam side down, in a buttered shallow ovenproof dish. Combine garlic and lemon juice and brush over chicken rolls. Sprinkle lightly with paprika, cover and bake for 40 to 45 minutes until tender. Chill. Cut into 5 mm (¼ in) slices.

Serve on bread rounds for a party savoury.

Note: The rolls may also be served whole as a main course with Provençale Sauce (see page 57).

MAKES 24

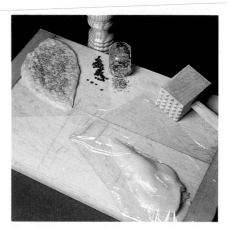

Put chicken, topside down, on a board and pound to 5 mm (¼ in) thickness.

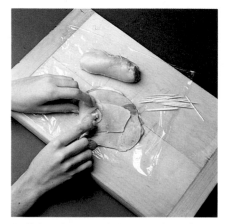

Roll lengthwise with ham inside and secure with toothpick.

Place seam side down in ovenproof dish, brush with combined garlic and lemon juice.

OPEN SANDWICHES

Good quality fresh ingredients combined with a neat, attractive presentation of contrasting textures and colours are important points for creating appetising open sandwiches.

16 slices black rye, Latvian sweet and sour, schinkenbrot or sunflower seed and barley bread

250 g (8 oz) butter or 1 quantity Avocado Butter (see recipe)

toppings of your choice

French dressing

TOPPINGS

1 *arugula*

thinly sliced Spanish (red) onions

sliced smoked chicken

snipped chives

chopped pecans or walnuts

cranberry sauce

2 *thinly sliced vine-ripened tomatoes*

sliced smoked chicken

shredded lettuce mixed with sliced spring onions (shallots)

wholegrain mustard

3 *sliced avocado brushed with lemon juice*

mignonette lettuce leaf

sliced chicken

cranberry sauce

pine nuts

4 *mignonette lettuce leaf*

chopped avocado tossed with lemon juice

chopped chicken

pine nuts

mayonnaise

Spread bread with softened butter or Avocado Butter. Place toppings on neatly in given order, making 4 of each variety. Sprinkle each open sandwich with 1 to 2 teaspoons French dressing. Serve immediately for a light snack or meal with extra salad greens if liked.

SUFFICIENT FOR 16 SANDWICHES

AVOCADO BUTTER

1 large avocado peeled and seeded

2 tablespoons fresh lime or lemon juice

250 g (8 oz) butter, softened

¼ teaspoon ground ginger

Purée avocado with other ingredients and chill. Any left over will freeze well.

Spread each slice of bread with Avocado Butter, top with selected topping.

AVOCADOS

If leaving sliced avocado exposed to air, brush lightly with lemon juice to help prevent discolouration.

CHICKEN SANDWICH FILLINGS

CHICKEN AND ALMOND

250 g (8 oz) finely chopped cooked chicken

60 g (2 oz) finely chopped celery

25 g (1 oz) ground almonds

3 tablespoons mayonnaise

CHICKEN AND CELERY

250 g (8 oz) finely chopped cooked chicken

125 g (4 oz) finely chopped celery

1 tablespoon finely chopped green or red capsicum (pepper)

4 tablespoons mayonnaise

CHICKEN AND HAM

250 g (8 oz) finely chopped cooked chicken

125 g (4 oz) finely chopped cooked ham

30 g (1 oz) finely chopped celery

4 tablespoons mayonnaise

1 tablespoon wholegrain mustard

Use a food processor or electric blender to prepare filling ingredients, or leave chicken in small, chunky pieces if preferred.

Mix all ingredients for chosen filling together thoroughly. Refrigerate, covered, until required. Use for enclosed or open sandwiches. Butter is not required on the bread when the chicken filling is moist, resulting in a healthier, low-fat sandwich.

MAKES 2 CUPS

CLUB MED SANDWICHES

24 slices warm buttered wholegrain toast, crusts removed

8 slices cooked chicken

mayonnaise

8 small crisp lettuce leaves

8 rashers crisp fried bacon, halved with rind removed

16 slices vine-ripened tomato

8 tablespoons sun dried tomatoes in oil, drained

Cover 8 slices of toast with chicken, spread with mayonnaise and cover each with lettuce and another slice of toast. Spread these with mayonnaise and arrange the slices of bacon, 2 slices of tomato and 1 tablespoon sun dried tomatoes on top of each. Cover with remaining slice of toast and fasten securely with toothpicks. Cut each sandwich diagonally into 2 triangles.

Serve sandwiches garnished with salad greens for a substantial snack.

SERVES 8

Open sandwiches

CRUNCHY CHICKEN SPREAD

This spread is ideal for a 'Champagne and Chicken Sandwich' celebration.

250 g (8 oz) chopped cooked chicken

60 g (2 oz) finely chopped celery

60 g (2 oz) finely chopped apple

3 tablespoons mayonnaise

1 tablespoon mango chutney

salt and pepper

1 teaspoon fresh lemon juice

4 slices white bread

4 slices wholegrain bread

butter for spreading

Combine chicken, celery and apple with mayonnaise and chutney. Blend in food processor or electric blender briefly. Mixture should still be crunchy. Season to taste with salt, pepper and lemon juice. Refrigerate until required. To serve, spread chicken mixture on buttered white bread, top with wholegrain bread, and cut into small squares or fingers.

MAKES APPROXIMATELY 16

CHICKEN LIVER PATE

375 g (12 oz) chicken livers

3 rashers bacon

1 onion, chopped

125 g (4 oz) butter

2 teaspoons brandy

2 teaspoons port

salt and pepper

Clean livers. Cut rind and any bones off bacon and cut bacon into strips. Cook bacon and rind in a frying pan over low heat until all the fat has run out. Add chicken livers and onion and cook, stirring, for 5 minutes.

Discard bacon rinds and purée chicken mixture with butter, brandy and port in a food processor or electric blender. Season to taste with salt and pepper. Pour into dish and refrigerate until set.

Serve on savoury biscuits for a picnic or with fingers of toast for a first course or a party savoury.

SERVES 8 TO 12

TERIYAKI CHICKEN WINGS

Use a commercial marinade for this tasty dish.

1 kg (2 lb) chicken wings

1 cup (250 ml/8 fl oz) teriyaki marinade

2 tablespoons dry sherry or mirin

1 tablespoon honey

2 cloves garlic, crushed

Preheat oven to 190°C (375°F).

Trim off and discard chicken wing tips, remove any excess skin and fat. Mix teriyaki marinade with sherry, honey and garlic. Pour over chicken wings, cover and marinate in refrigerator overnight. Arrange chicken in a single layer in a baking dish/roasting tin and cook in an oven for 40 to 45 minutes or until cooked, basting occasionally.

Serve hot for a party savoury or for a picnic.

SERVES 8

CHICKEN LEGS IN FILO

4 tablespoons grated Parmesan cheese

60 g (2 oz) grated tasty cheese

1 teaspoon dried oregano

12 chicken drumsticks, skinned and excess fat removed

60 g (2 oz) butter, melted

12 sheets filo pastry

Preheat oven to 190°C (375°F).

Mix the cheeses and oregano together. Brush drumsticks with butter and coat with cheese mixture.

Brush a sheet of filo with butter, keeping remainder of filo covered with a damp cloth. Place drumstick on pastry and roll up like a bag. Brush each parcel with butter and arrange in a shallow greased ovenproof dish.

Bake for 35 minutes or until chicken is tender.

Serve as a first course accompanied by salad greens or serve for a picnic.

SERVES 12

GRATED PARMESAN

Freshly grated parmesan has a much nicer flavour than commercially grated cheese. Buy parmesan in a block from your delicatessen and grate as required.

Chicken Legs in Filo

FINGER LICKING CHICKEN 23

FOCACCIA WITH CHICKEN AND SUN DRIED TOMATOES

Tomato pâté is available in leading delicatessen stores.

1 piece focaccia 15 x 10 cm (6 x 4 in)

2 tablespoons light olive oil

1 clove garlic, crushed

tomato pâté for spreading

crisp cos lettuce leaves

1 vine-ripe tomato, sliced

sliced cooked chicken breast

2 tablespoons sun dried tomatoes in oil

Slice focaccia through centre and brush inside surfaces with olive oil mixed with garlic. Place under a medium—hot grill, oil side upwards, and grill until golden and crisp.

Spread toasted side of bottom slice of focaccia with tomato pâté. Top with lettuce leaves, slices of tomato and cooked chicken, then drained sun-dried tomatoes in oil.

Place top slice of focaccia on top of filling and serve accompanied by a side salad of mixed salad greens.

SERVES 1

LOW FAT CHICKEN

Remove skin from chicken pieces to reduce fat, cholesterol and kilojoules.

Skin is easily removed from chicken pieces. Simply ease fingertips under skin and pull.

Focaccia with Chicken and Sun Dried Tomatoes

RUMAKI

FOR EACH NIBBLE ALLOW:

1 chicken liver lobe or segment

butter for frying

½ water chestnut, drained

½ rasher bacon, rind and bones removed

Clean and separate chicken livers. Melt a little butter in a frying pan and gently cook livers until colour changes. Cool. Then wrap 1 piece chicken liver with ½ water chestnut in ½ rasher bacon. Fasten with a toothpick or thread onto bamboo skewers and refrigerate until needed. To cook, grill until bacon is crisp.

Serve immediately as party finger food.

TASTY CHICKEN BITES

6 chicken breast fillets, skinned

60 g (2 oz) butter

1 tablespoon plain (all-purpose) flour

1 teaspoon dried tarragon

1 teaspoon lemon pepper

¼ teaspoon salt

½ cup (125 ml/4 fl oz) chicken stock

1 tablespoon French mustard

3 thin slices lemon, halved

1 tablespoon finely chopped parsley

Cut each breast into 6 to 8 bite-sized pieces. Melt butter in a large frying pan, add chicken and sprinkle with flour, tarragon, lemon pepper and salt.

Cook 5 minutes, stirring constantly. Add stock, mustard and lemon; stir. Cover and cook 2 to 3 minutes. Sprinkle with parsley and serve with cocktail sticks.

Serve for a party savoury or at a picnic.

MAKES APPROXIMATELY 36

CHICKEN PECAN TURNOVERS

1 small onion, grated

15 g (½ oz) butter

250 g (8 oz) chopped cooked chicken

30 g (1 oz) chopped pecans

2 tablespoons yoghurt

1 egg, beaten

2 tablespoons shredded fresh basil

½ teaspoon salt

freshly ground black pepper

1 x 5 sheet packet puff pastry

¼ cup (60 ml/2 fl oz) milk for glazing

Preheat oven to 200°C (400°F).

Cook onion gently in butter for 5 minutes. Mix with the chicken, pecans, yoghurt, egg, basil and seasoning.

Cut ten 7 cm (2¾ in) diameter circles from each sheet of pastry. Place a teaspoon of mixture in centre of each circle. Brush edges with milk and fold over. Press edges together lightly and brush tops with milk.

Arrange on baking trays and bake for 20 minutes until golden and cooked.

Serve for a picnic or packed lunch.

MAKES 50

FRENCH FRIED SANDWICHES

4 chicken sandwiches using 8 slices of white or wholegrain bread

2 eggs, lightly beaten

60 g (2 oz) plain (all-purpose) flour

½ teaspoon salt

freshly ground black pepper

1 cup (250 ml/8 fl oz) milk

oil for deep frying

Prepare sandwiches. Combine remaining ingredients and beat until smooth. Dip sandwiches into batter and deep fry at 190°C (375°F) until browned. Drain well on kitchen paper towels.

Serve sandwiches hot accompanied by a light salad garnish if liked.

SERVES 4

CHICKEN BALLS WITH CREAMY MANGO SAUCE

250 g (8 oz) cream cheese

250 g (8 oz) finely chopped or minced cooked chicken

125 g (4 oz) chopped almonds

2 tablespoons mayonnaise

1 tablespoon curry powder or paste

1 tablespoon mango chutney

45 g (1½ oz) desiccated coconut, toasted

CREAMY MANGO SAUCE

1½ cups (300 ml/10 fl oz) sour cream

1 cup (250 ml/8 fl oz) mayonnaise

2 cloves garlic, crushed

¼ cup mango chutney

Beat cheese with an electric mixer until soft. Add all ingredients except coconut. Mix and roll into 36 balls. Roll in coconut and chill. These balls can be prepared in advance and refrigerated or frozen.

To make sauce: Blend all sauce ingredients together. Pour into a small serving bowl and chill for 1 hour

Serve Chicken Balls with cocktail sticks and offer the sauce for dipping for a party.

MAKES 36 BALLS

Soups

*S*teaming bowls of delicious soups are always a winter favourite but more and more often now we see soups served chilled as well. Chilled soup is a refreshing change on a summer-time table. Recipes for both soups are included in this section.

CHICKEN STOCK

This stock may be made in a pressure cooker in 30 minutes to save time but reduce liquid to 4 cups (1 litre/32 fl oz).

- *1 uncooked chicken carcass, or equivalent bones and giblets*
- *1 onion, stuck with 2 cloves*
- *1 carrot, sliced*
- *outside stalks of washed head of celery or 1 leek, sliced*
- *1 bay leaf*
- *3 stems parsley*
- *1 teaspoon salt*
- *¼ teaspoon pepper*
- *5 cups (1¼ litres/40 fl oz) water*

Place all the ingredients in a large pan, cover with the water and bring to the boil slowly.

Using a slotted spoon, remove any scum from the surface then, when the liquid comes back to the boil, cover and boil gently for 2 hours, then strain, season to taste with salt and pepper and cool.

Refrigerate the stock until surface fat solidifies, then skim this off. Use within 3 days, or freeze.

MAKES APPROXIMATELY 1 LITRE (32 FL OZ)

FREEZING STOCK

Before freezing, make sure your stock cools down as fast as possible (reducing the risk of bacterial growth) by putting it into pre-chilled containers.

Dishes on previous pages: Cream of Carrot Soup (page 34), Thai Chicken and Coconut Soup (page 34)

MEXICAN CHICKEN BROTH

- *1 x 1.5 kg (3 lb) chicken*
- *8 cups (2 litres/64 fl oz) water*
- *1 bouquet garni (parsley, thyme, bay leaf)*
- *2 carrots, sliced*
- *3 stalks celery, sliced*
- *1 onion, chopped*
- *1 green capsicum (pepper) seeded and chopped*
- *1 clove garlic, crushed*
- *3 potatoes, peeled and cubed*
- *1 cup green peas*
- *¼ cup (60 ml/2 fl oz) taco sauce*
- *1 tablespoon chopped fresh coriander leaves or ¼ teaspoon ground coriander (cilantro)*
- *¼ teaspoon cumin seeds, crushed*
- *2 teaspoons salt*

Cook chicken in water with bouquet garni as for Chicken and Corn Chowder (see recipe page 30). Lift out chicken and allow to cool. Cool stock and skim off fat. Remove bouquet garni. Add carrots, celery, onion, capsicum and garlic to stock. Cover and simmer 30 minutes. Remove chicken meat from carcass, discard skin and chop meat. Add remaining ingredients and chicken meat to broth, cover and simmer for a further 30 minutes until vegetables are tender. Check seasoning before serving.

Serve broth hot with corn bread.

SERVES 6 TO 8

BOUQUET GARNI

Prepare a bouquet garni by tying together a sprig of parsley, a bay leaf and a piece of celery studded with peppercorns. Other herbs may also be used. Alternatively, commercially prepared bouquet garnis are available from your supermarket.

PARSLEY SOUP

This soup is rich in vitamin C and can be enjoyed all year round.

- *90 g (3 oz) chopped fresh parsley*
- *4 cups (1 litre/32 fl oz) chicken stock*
- *30 g (1 oz) butter*
- *1 large onion, finely chopped*
- *2 tablespoons plain (all-purpose) flour*
- *salt and pepper*
- *1 large potato, peeled and finely diced*
- *¾ cup (180 ml/6 fl oz) milk*

Add parsley to the stock, bring to the boil and simmer 10 minutes. Purée in blender or food processor.

Melt butter and gently fry onion until soft. Stir in flour; cook for 1 minute stirring continuously. Gradually add puréed stock, stirring constantly. Season to taste. Bring to the boil, stirring constantly. Cook potato in milk for 15 minutes until tender. Add to soup and heat through gently.

Serve soup hot accompanied by wholemeal bread rolls.

SERVES 4 TO 6

SPEEDY STOCK

A pressure cooker will also help you to produce a good flavoured stock in a minimum time.

Mexican Chicken Broth

PUMPKIN SOUP

30 g (1 oz) butter

1 onion, finely chopped

500 g (1 lb) pumpkin, peeled and chopped

3 cups (750 ml/24 fl oz) chicken stock

pinch ground nutmeg

salt and pepper

½ cup (125 ml/4 fl oz) milk

½ cup (125 ml/4 fl oz) cream

1 tablespoon finely chopped parsley or snipped chives to garnish

Melt butter in a medium-sized pan. Add onion and fry gently for 2 to 3 minutes. Add pumpkin and stock and simmer 30 minutes until pumpkin is tender.

Purée in a food processor or blender and season to taste with nutmeg, salt and pepper. Stir in milk and cream and garnish with parsley or chives.

Serve soup hot with warm damper or soft bread rolls.

SERVES 6

COCONUT PRAWN (SHRIMP) SOUP

60 g (2 oz) butter

4 sliced spring onions (shallots)

1 leek, washed and thinly sliced

2 tablespoons plain (all-purpose) flour

4 cups (1 litre/32 fl oz) chicken stock

3 tablespoons tomato paste

16 chopped green prawns (shrimps), shelled and deveined

½ cup (125 ml/4 fl oz) coconut milk

freshly ground black pepper

1 tablespoon chopped chives or coriander (cilantro) leaves to garnish

Melt butter in a large pan, add spring onions and leek and cook gently until soft. Add flour and stir over a medium heat for 1 minute. Pour in stock and bring to the boil, stirring constantly. Add tomato paste, prawns, coconut milk and season to taste. Simmer gently just until prawns turn orange in colour and are cooked through. Overcooking will toughen the prawns. Garnish with chives or coriander.

Serve hot with naan (Indian bread) or soft bread rolls.

SERVES 4 TO 6

SHELLING PRAWNS (SHRIMPS)

To shell green prawns, first remove the head, then the tail, squeezing gently so you don't tear the meat. Peel the remainder of the shell off with the legs. Make a small slit along the back of the prawn and remove the dark vein.

CHICKEN AND CORN CHOWDER

1 x 1.5 kg (3 lb) boiling fowl

8 cups (2 litres/64 fl oz) water

1 large onion, chopped

1 clove garlic, crushed

125 g (4 oz) diced celery

1 x 440 g (14 oz) can sweetcorn kernels, drained

salt

¼ teaspoon pepper

1 packet saffron threads

1 cup chopped fresh parsley

155 g (5 oz) pasta noodles

Place fowl in large pan, add water and bring to the boil. Remove scum. Cover and simmer 2 hours or until fowl is tender enough to pierce easily with a fork. Lift out fowl and leave to cool. Strain stock and skim off as much fat as possible, or leave in freezer to allow fat to set.

Add onion, garlic and celery to the stock, cover and simmer 30 minutes. Add corn, salt, pepper and saffron, cover and simmer a further 10 minutes.

Skin chicken, strip meat from bones and cut into bite-sized pieces. Return chicken meat to stock with parsley. Add noodles, and boil, covered, stirring occasionally for 12 to 15 minutes until the noodles are tender. Adjust seasoning to taste.

Serve soup hot accompanied by warm crusty bread rolls.

SERVES 8

Pumpkin Soup, Chicken and Corn Chowder, and Coconut Prawn Soup

SPICY CHICKEN AND CUCUMBER SOUP

60 g (2 oz) butter

2 large cucumbers, peeled, seeded and chopped

1 French shallot, thinly sliced

½ teaspoon chopped ginger root

½ teaspoon chopped chilli

4 cups (1 litre/32 fl oz) chicken stock

1 tablespoon chopped fresh mint

1 teaspoon chopped fresh thyme

salt and pepper

1 cup (250 ml/8 fl oz) yoghurt

croûtons for serving

Melt butter in a large pan. Add cucumber and shallot and cook gently until softened. Add ginger and chilli. Stir in stock, herbs and salt and pepper to taste. Bring to the boil, remove from heat.

Blend a little of the hot stock with the yoghurt and add to the remaining soup stirring until combined. Heat through but do not allow to boil.

Serve soup with croûtons.

SERVES 8

TO MAKE CROUTONS

Make croûtons by frying quarters of crustless bread in butter and oil. Drain on crumpled kitchen paper. Try dipping the ends in chopped parsley.

ITALIAN MUSHROOM SOUP

1 tablespoon olive oil

30 g (1 oz) butter

1 onion, grated

1 clove garlic, peeled and halved

500 g (1 lb) mushrooms, thinly sliced

3 tablespoons tomato paste

3 cups (750 ml/24 fl oz) chicken stock

2 tablespoons sweet vermouth or dry sherry

salt and pepper

4 egg yolks

2 tablespoons finely chopped parsley

3 tablespoons grated Parmesan cheese

4 slices crusty bread, toasted and buttered

Heat oil and butter in a large pan and gently fry onion and garlic until lightly browned. Remove garlic. Stir in mushrooms and cook 5 minutes. Stir in tomato paste and mix well. Add chicken stock and vermouth and season to taste with salt and pepper. Simmer 10 minutes.

Beat together egg yolks, parsley and Parmesan cheese. Beat into gently boiling soup with a wire whisk.

Serve hot soup at once over toasted bread.

SERVES 4

MUSHROOMS

To clean mushrooms, wipe with a damp cloth. Don't wash under water and don't peel the skin off as this is the most nutritious part of the mushroom.

CHICKEN AND ALMOND SOUP

1 cup (155 g/5 oz) blanched almonds

4 sliced spring onions (shallots)

6 cups (1.5 litres/48 fl oz) chicken stock

salt and pepper

2 tablespoons chopped fresh coriander (cilantro) or 1 teaspoon crushed coriander seeds

½ cup (125 ml/4 fl oz) sour cream

2 egg yolks

grated rind of ½ lemon

To toast the almonds spread evenly on a baking tray, place in a 150°C (300°F) oven and bake for 10 minutes or until a light straw colour.

Combine almonds with spring onions in a food processor or blender and process until they form a smooth paste. Add to stock in a large pan and bring to the boil. Season to taste with salt and pepper, add coriander and simmer for 15 minutes.

Beat together sour cream and egg yolks and blend with a little hot stock, then add to soup, stirring constantly over low heat until thickened. Do not boil. Add lemon rind just before serving.

Serve soup accompanied by warm, torn pita bread or damper rolls.

SERVES 8

Spicy Chicken and Cucumber Soup, Italian Mushroom Soup and Chicken and Almond Soup

CREAM OF CARROT SOUP

6 medium carrots, peeled and chopped

1 small onion, chopped

1 bay leaf

40 g (1⅓ oz) butter

3 cups (750 ml/24 fl oz) chicken stock

1/2 cup (125 ml/4 fl oz) cream

salt and pepper

1 tablespoon grated lemon rind

1 tablespoon chopped parsley

Combine carrots, onion, bay leaf and butter in a large pan. Cover and cook over low heat for 5 minutes, add 1 cup stock and simmer until carrots are tender. Remove bay leaf and add another cup of stock.

Purée in food processor or electric blender. Return to pan and add remaining stock. Stir in cream. Season to taste with salt and pepper and garnish with lemon rind and parsley.

Serve hot accompanied by warm French bread.

SERVES 4 TO 6

THAI CHICKEN AND COCONUT SOUP

A popular soup in Thai restaurants which is easy to prepare at home.

4 small chicken breast fillets

2 x 410 g (13 fl oz) cans coconut milk

2 cups (500 ml/16 fl oz) water or lightly flavoured chicken stock

2 tablespoons grated ginger

1 onion, finely chopped

2 stalks lemon grass, sliced

2 tablespoons chopped coriander (cilantro) roots and stems

1 tablespoon fish sauce or salt to taste

4 sliced spring onions (shallots)

4 red chillies, seeded and thinly sliced

3 tablespoons fresh lime juice

2 tablespoons shredded coriander (cilantro) leaves (extra)

strips of lime rind and coriander leaves to garnish

Trim chicken and cut into thin strips. Place in a pan with 1 can coconut milk, 1 cup water or stock, ginger, onion, lemon grass and coriander roots and stems.

Cover and bring to the boil then simmer for 10 minutes. Add remaining coconut milk and water, and return to the boil. Stir in fish sauce, spring onions, red chillies, lime juice and coriander leaves and remove from heat.

Serve hot soup immediately garnished with lime rind and coriander leaves.

SERVES 6

COCK-A-LEEKIE

2.5 kg (5 lb) chicken

4 cups (1 litre/32 fl oz) chicken stock

1 bouquet garni

½ cup (90 g/3 oz) pearl barley

6 slim leeks, trimmed and thoroughly washed

12 prunes, pitted and soaked

2 tablespoons chopped parsley

1 teaspoon salt

freshly ground black pepper

½ cup (125 ml/4 fl oz) cream, optional

Simmer chicken in a large, covered pan with stock, bouquet garni and barley for 40 minutes.

Slice leeks and add them, with the prunes, and cook for a further 15 minutes.

Discard the bouquet garni, and lift out the chicken. Skin and bone chicken and cut the meat into bite-sized pieces, return these to the pan.

Chill soup then skim fat from the surface. Reheat soup then add parsley and salt and pepper to taste. Stir in cream if liked, simmer until heated through.

Serve soup hot with baps or soft bread rolls.

SERVES 6 TO 8

AVGOLEMONO

5 cups (1.25 litres/40 fl oz) good flavoured chicken stock

70 g (2½ oz) long grain rice

2 eggs

juice 1 lemon

salt and pepper

6 lemon slices

Bring chicken stock to the boil, stir in rice and simmer about 15 to 20 minutes until rice is tender.

Beat eggs and lemon juice together in a bowl until well blended.

Gradually stir a little (about 2 tablespoons) of the boiling stock into the egg and lemon mixture. Then add 2 cups stock and stir until it is slightly thickened. Whisk combined mixture back into remaining stock and heat through. Do not boil or the soup will curdle.

Season to taste with salt and pepper.

Serve soup hot with lemon slices and torn pita bread.

SERVES 6

CHILLED AVOCADO SOUP

2 avocados

1 cup (250 ml/8 fl oz) chicken stock

4 sliced spring onions (shallots)

½ cup (125 ml/4 fl oz) light sour cream

½ cup (125 ml/4 fl oz) natural yoghurt

2 tablespoons lemon juice

1 teaspoon Tabasco sauce

½ teaspoon salt

chopped parsley to garnish

Scoop out avocado flesh and purée with remaining ingredients in a food processor or electric blender. Chill for 1 hour before serving. Add more stock if soup is too thick, as consistency will vary according to type of avocado used. Garnish with chopped parsley.

Serve chilled.

SERVES 4

COLD CHICKEN AND APPLE SOUP

The hot and cold contrast creates the element of surprise in this unusual summer soup that can also be served hot in cooler weather.

30 g (1 oz) butter or ghee

1 large onion, chopped

2 stalks celery with green tops, sliced

1 tablespoon curry powder

3 tablespoons plain (all-purpose) flour

2 large green apples, cored and roughly chopped

250 g (8 oz) cooked chicken chopped

5 cups (1.25 litres/40 fl oz) chicken stock

1 tablespoon fresh lemon juice

salt and pepper to taste

natural yoghurt or cream

chopped chives to garnish

Melt butter in a large pan and cook onion and celery for about 5 minutes until softened. Add curry powder and flour and cook for 2 minutes, stirring occasionally. Add apple, chicken and 1 cup stock and simmer for 5 minutes. Cool slightly.

Purée mixture in a food processor or blender. This may need to be done in several batches. Return purée to pan and add remaining chicken stock, lemon juice, salt and pepper. Bring to boil and simmer for about 10 minutes to bring out the flavour.

Cool soup then cover and chill in refrigerator. Serve cold with a spoonful of yoghurt or cream in each bowl and a sprinkle of chopped chives.

SERVES 4 TO 6

CHILLED WATERCRESS SOUP

1 kg (2 lb) potatoes, peeled and sliced

2 large leeks, washed and sliced

1½ bunches watercress, washed

4 cups (1 litre/32 fl oz) chicken stock

1 ham bone

salt

freshly ground black pepper

1¼ cups (300 ml/10 fl oz) cream

sprigs of watercress to garnish

Combine potatoes, leeks, watercress, stock and ham bone in a large pan and cook for 10 minutes or until the potatoes are just tender. Remove ham bone and cut the ham from the bone. Purée vegetables, stock and ham in a food processor or blender and season to taste with salt and pepper. Chill.

Just before serving, lightly whip cream and fold through soup or add a dollop to individual bowls.

Serve soup chilled garnished with sprigs of watercress.

SERVES 6

Meals in Minutes

*I*f you dash home after a busy day with a barbecued take-away chicken for the family dinner but lack inspirational ideas for what to serve with it, then this chapter is for you. There are a few recipes that can be prepared the night before, still using cooked chopped chicken, and popped in the oven for 30 minutes or heated quickly in a microwave oven. These recipes will be invaluable to busy people.

SAMBALS

These are side dishes which make good accompaniments for curries and vindaloos. Try some of these ideas:

• Mix low fat natural yoghurt with chopped cucumber and fresh mint.

• Combine sliced bananas with chopped chilli and lemon juice, or use apple instead of banana.

• Mix 1 cup coconut milk with chopped onion, crushed garlic and chilli powder.

• Make up your own selection of vegetables, blanch them and combine with chopped chillies, lemon juice, a little oil and desiccated coconut.

Dishes on previous pages: Chicken Pizza (page 46), Neapolitan Chicken (page 39)

INDONESIAN CHICKEN CURRY

2 tablespoons peanut oil

1 large onion, thinly sliced

2 tablespoons curry powder or paste

1 x 410 g (13 oz) can tomatoes

1¾ cups (420 ml/14 fl oz) coconut milk

2 teaspoon brown sugar

2 tablespoons crunchy peanut butter

1 tablespoon mango chutney

2 cups chopped cooked chicken

Heat oil in a large frying pan and gently fry onion until soft. Add curry powder and stir over a medium heat for 2 minutes. Add tomatoes, coconut milk, sugar, peanut butter and chutney and stir until peanut butter melts and sauce comes to the boil. Add chicken, cover and simmer for 5 to 10 minutes until heated through and sauce has thickened.

Serve hot with rice and curry accompaniments (sambals) such as diced tomato and cucumber in oil and vinegar dressing and sliced banana and shredded coconut in natural yoghurt and pappadums.

SERVES 4

CRUSHED GARLIC

Crush garlic cloves by chopping finely and then pressing with the blade of a knife to crush. A little salt sprinkled onto the clove before crushing will absorb any garlic juice that escapes. Alternatively, use a garlic press.

SWEET AND SOUR CHICKEN

1 x 1.5 kg (3 lb) barbecued chicken

SAUCE

2 tablespoons safflower oil

2 cloves garlic, crushed

1 onion, cut into 12 wedges

1 carrot, thinly sliced diagonally

1 green capsicum (pepper), sliced

125 ml (4 fl oz) pineapple cubes, optional

3 tablespoons raw or brown sugar

3 tablespoons white vinegar

1 tablespoon light soy sauce

1 cup (250 ml/8 fl oz) chicken stock

1 tablespoon cornflour (cornstarch)

2 tablespoons cold water

Cut backbone and wing tips from chicken, then cut chicken into small chunky pieces 'Chinese style'.

Sauce: In a wok or large frying pan, heat oil and stir-fry garlic and onion until soft and transparent. Add carrot and capsicum and stir-fry for 2 minutes. Add pineapple if used, sugar, vinegar, soy sauce and stock, bring to the boil and simmer for 1 minute. Blend cornflour with cold water, add to wok and stir continuously until sauce thickens and clears. Add chicken pieces to sauce and heat through gently. Serve Sweet and Sour Chicken with rice.

SERVES 4

NEAPOLITAN CHICKEN

2 x 425 g (13½ oz) cans tomatoes, drained and roughly chopped

3 cloves garlic, crushed

1 tablespoon olive oil

1 tablespoon chopped fresh oregano or 1 teaspoon dried oregano

freshly ground black pepper

1 teaspoon brown sugar

¾ cup (180 ml/6 fl oz) white wine

1 x 1.5 kg (3 lb) cooked chicken

chopped parsley

Fry tomatoes and garlic in oil over a low heat for 5 minutes. Add oregano, pepper, brown sugar and wine, bring to the boil and simmer for 15 minutes. Cut the chicken into joints and discard backbone and wing tips. Add chicken pieces to sauce and heat through gently.

Serve hot sprinkled with chopped parsley accompanied with rice or pasta noodles and a green vegetable or salad.

SERVES 4 TO 6

COOKED CHICKEN

Half a barbecued chicken will yield 2 cups chopped cooked chicken.

QUICK CHICKEN MOUSSAKA

500 g (1 lb) eggplant (aubergine)

4 tablespoons olive oil

1 large onion, finely chopped

1 x 400 g (approximately 13 oz) can tomatoes

4 tablespoons tomato paste

2 tablespoons chopped continental parsley

500 g (1 lb) finely chopped cooked chicken

freshly ground black pepper

1 egg, beaten

1 x 200 g (6½ oz) carton natural yoghurt

Preheat oven to 180°C (350°F).

Cut eggplant into 1 cm (½ in) cubes and gently fry in 3 tablespoons oil, stirring occasionally until softened. Set aside. Heat remaining oil in pan and gently fry onion until soft. Stir in tomatoes, tomato paste and parsley, bring to the boil and simmer 5 minutes. Place half the eggplant in a casserole, cover with half the chicken, sprinkle with pepper and cover chicken with half the tomato mixture. Repeat layers and press down to smooth the top. Mix egg with yoghurt, spread over the top and cook in an oven for 30 minutes or until bubbling hot. Alternatively cook in a microwave oven on medium setting for 10 minutes.

Serve with multi-grain rice and a green salad.

SERVES 4

EGGPLANT (AUBERGINE)

When egglplants (aubergines) are sliced and salted, this is called 'degorging'. This process draws out moisture and any bitterness.

CHICKEN WITH SPICY SALSA

Select a mild, medium or hot taco sauce for this dish according to your taste.

1 x 1.5 kg (3 lb) barbecued chicken

2 tablespoons olive oil

2 white onions, sliced

1 sweet chilli pepper or yellow butter capsicum (pepper), sliced

1 cup (250 ml/8 fl oz) taco sauce

1 cup (250 ml/8 fl oz) tomato juice

toasted sesame seeds and warm corn chips to serve

Cut chicken into serving portions and discard backbone and wing tips. Heat oil in a large pan and gently fry onions and chilli peppers until soft. Stir in taco sauce and tomato juice and bring to the boil. Add chicken and heat through gently.

Serve Chicken with Spicy Salsa sprinkled with toasted sesame seeds and warm corn chips, accompanied by new potatoes or cornbread and salad.

SERVES 4

CHICKEN AND BROCCOLI MINI STRUDELS

90 g (3 oz) butter

1 onion, finely chopped

250 g (8 oz) chopped cooked chicken

1 cup broccoli florets, blanched

½ cup (125 g/4 oz) cottage cheese

½ cup (125 ml/4 fl oz) light sour cream

2 teaspoons wholegrain mustard

salt and pepper

8 sheets filo pastry

spring onions (shallots) to garnish

Preheat oven to 190°C (375°F).

Heat 30 g (1 oz) butter and gently fry onion until soft. Remove from heat and mix gently with chicken, broccoli, cottage cheese, sour cream and mustard. Season to taste with salt and pepper.

Melt remaining butter, brush over a sheet of filo pastry and top with another sheet of pastry. Cut pastry in half. Place an eighth of the chicken mixture along the short edge of each layered pastry half. Fold short edge over, then roll up neatly to form a cylinder.and squeeze ends to form a bon-bon (Christmas cracker) shape. Repeat with remaining filo and filling to make 8 mini strudels.

Place on a baking tray and brush with more melted butter. Bake for 15 minutes or until crisp and golden.

Cut shallots into long ribbon strips, scrape off inner membrane and place in iced water to curl up. Tie shallot ribbons around each end of mini strudels.

Serve hot with brown rice and grilled tomatoes.

SERVES 4

Chicken and Broccoli Mini Strudels

Chicken Réchauffé

CHICKEN RECHAUFFE

500 g (1 lb) chopped cooked chicken

500 g (1 lb) cooked green beans

185 g (6 oz) cooked white rice (60 g (2 oz) raw)

185 g (6 oz) cooked brown rice (60 g (2 oz) raw)

½ cup (125 ml/4 fl oz) mayonnaise or natural yoghurt

60 g (2 oz) sliced celery

2 tablespoons chopped red capsicum (pepper)

2 tablespoons finely chopped onion

salt and pepper

1 x 430 g (14 oz) can cream of celery soup

paprika

Preheat oven to 180°C (350°F).

Mix all ingredients together except paprika, blending with soup. Pour into a casserole, sprinkle with paprika and bake for 25 minutes until heated through. Alternatively, the dish can be heated in the microwave oven on high for 10 to 12 minutes.

Serve hot accompanied by a crisp green salad.

SERVES 4 TO 6

CREAMY STUFFED MUSHROOMS

16 large mushroom cups

⅔ cup finely chopped onion

60 g (2 oz) butter

2 cups chopped cooked chicken

½ cup (125 ml/4 fl oz) white wine

½ teaspoon Worcestershire sauce, optional

pinch of grated nutmeg

salt and pepper

1 egg, beaten

1 cup fresh breadcrumbs

extra 60 g (2 oz) butter

30 g (1 oz) grated Parmesan cheese

CREAM SAUCE

30 g (1 oz) butter

1 tablespoon plain (all-purpose) flour

1 cup (250 ml/8 fl oz) milk

salt and pepper

Preheat oven to 180°C (350°F).

Remove stems from mushrooms and chop sufficient stems to measure ⅔ cup. Cook stems with onion in butter until soft. Stir in chicken and cook for 5 minutes. Add wine, Worcestershire sauce if liked, nutmeg and salt and pepper to taste and simmer for 5 minutes. Remove from heat and stir in egg, cream sauce and breadcrumbs. Simmer for 5 minutes.

Lightly cook mushroom cups in extra butter skin side down, for 2 to 3 minutes. Fill with chicken mixture. Sprinkle with Parmesan cheese and bake for 10 to 15 minutes until cheese browns. (Any leftover filling can be heated and served on toast.)

To make the cream sauce, melt butter in a saucepan, stir in flour and cook for 1 minute. Gradually add milk, stirring constantly, and bring to the boil stirring continuously until thickened. Season to taste with salt and pepper.

Serve with small new potatoes (chats) and green salad.

Note: The sauce can be made in a microwave oven. The filling can be prepared in advance. Fill mushroom cups and bake just before serving.

MAKES 16, SERVES 4

MUSHROOM FILLINGS

Alternative mushroom fillings can be used. Try these:

• Cook the mushroom stems with a small amount of chopped onion and garlic in a pan with a little olive oil. Add chopped chicken, tomato, capsicum (pepper), oregano and parsley. Season to taste with plenty of freshly ground black pepper. Fill the mushroom cups and sprinkle with Parmesan cheese before placing under the griller.

• Make Creamy Stuffed Mushrooms as directed but add a can of crabmeat or some cooked asparagus with the chicken.

SWISS CHICKEN

This recipe can be halved to serve 4 people.

125 g (4 oz) chopped onion

30 g (1 oz) butter

1kg (2lb) chopped cooked chicken

250 g (8 oz) chopped celery

1 cup (250 ml/8 fl oz) light sour cream

½ cup (125 ml/4 fl oz) milk

250 g (8 oz) Swiss cheese, grated or shredded

½ teaspoon salt

freshly ground black pepper

30 g (1 oz) toasted slivered almonds

2 cups toasted bread cubes

Preheat oven to 180°C (350°F).

Cook onion gently in butter until soft. Combine all ingredients except almonds and bread cubes. Pour into 2 litre (64 fl oz) casserole and sprinkle with almonds and bread cubes. Bake for 30 minutes or until bubbling hot or microwave on high for 10 minutes.

Serve hot with rice or pasta noodles and red cabbage coleslaw.

SERVES 8

TOASTED ALMONDS

To toast almonds, spread onto an oven tray and put in a hot oven until golden.

CHICKEN AND ASPARAGUS CREPES

12 pre-cooked crêpes (see recipe)

60 g (2 oz) butter

1 small onion, chopped

125 g (4 oz) mushrooms, sliced

3 tablespoons plain (all-purpose) flour

⅔ cup (160 ml/5½ fl oz) chicken stock

½ cup (125 ml/4 fl oz) milk or cream

500 g (1 lb) diced, cooked chicken

250 g (8 oz) asparagus spears, cooked and sliced

60 g (2 oz) grated Parmesan cheese

1 teaspoon chopped fresh thyme

½ teaspoon salt

freshly ground black pepper

60 g (2 oz) grated Cheddar cheese

Preheat oven to 180°C (350°F).

Melt butter in frying pan, add onion and mushrooms and cook gently until tender. Mix in flour and cook for 1 minute stirring without browning. Add chicken stock and milk, stirring until the sauce boils and thickens.

Remove from heat and stir in diced chicken, asparagus, Parmesan cheese, thyme, salt and pepper and leave to cool.

Place a little filling along the middle of each crêpe and roll up. Arrange filled crepes in a single layer in a shallow oblong dish, cover with aluminium foil and bake for 20 to 30 minutes to heat through. Remove foil, sprinkle with cheese and bake uncovered until the cheese melts.

Allow 2 crêpes per serving.

Note: This dish can be completely prepared in advance, covered and kept refrigerated overnight.

SERVES 6

CREPES (PANCAKES)

The pancake batter may be made in a food processor or blender.

125 g (4 oz) plain (all-purpose) flour

½ teaspoon salt

2 eggs, beaten

1¼ cups (300 ml/10 fl oz) milk

1 teaspoon melted butter

60 g (2 oz) butter for frying

Sift flour and salt into a mixing bowl. Make a well in the centre. In a separate bowl mix eggs, 1 cup milk and melted butter and pour into well. Stir flour gradually into liquid with a wooden spoon and beat lightly until batter is smooth and light. Refrigerate for an hour or so. If batter is too thick, add extra ¼ cup milk.

To make the pancakes, heat a little butter in a 17 cm (6¾ in) crêpe pan and pour off any excess. Using a jug, pour about 3 tablespoons batter into pan. Rotate the pan quickly to coat the bottom. Heat gently and when small bubbles appear turn the pancake. Cook for 1 minute on the other side.

Slide pancake out onto a plate. Layer pancakes between strips of greaseproof paper until all batter is cooked. Use as required.

CREPES

Crêpes can be made ahead of time. Store in an airtight container in the refrigerator.

CREPE FILLINGS

Alternative crêpe fillings can be used. Try these:

• Melt butter in frying pan and sauté onion.
Add flour and cook for 1 minute.
Add chicken stock and milk, stirring until thick.
Stir in chopped cooked chicken, chopped cooked bacon, blanched beans and toasted slivered almonds.
Season to taste with black pepper.

• Melt butter as above and sauté onion.
Add flour and mustard to taste and cook for 1 minute.
Add chicken stock and milk, stirring until thick.
Stir in chopped cooked chicken, diced ham, mushrooms and celery.
Season to taste with pepper.

• Sauté onion and garlic in a pan with a little olive oil.
Add chopped cooked chicken, diced eggplant (aubergine), mushrooms, tomato and capsicum (pepper).
Cook until the vegetables are softened slightly.
Add chicken stock mixed with a little cornflour.
Stir until sauce thickens.
Add chopped parsley, black pepper and any other herbs you like.
Use this filling in wholemeal pancakes.

SPINACH CHICKEN ENCHILADAS

Vacuum-packed tortillas may be used to save time.

> *500 g (1 lb) bunch spinach*
>
> *2 cups (500 ml/16 fl oz) chicken stock*
>
> *1 clove garlic, crushed*
>
> *1 x 440 g (14 oz) can cream of mushroom soup*
>
> *2 teaspoons chopped chillies*
>
> *1 tablespoon cornflour (cornstarch)*
>
> *1 large onion, finely chopped*
>
> *250 g (8 oz) mushrooms, sliced*
>
> *500 g (1 lb) cottage cheese*
>
> *80 g (2½ oz) chopped olives*
>
> *500 g (1 lb) chopped cooked chicken*
>
> *12 tortillas (see recipe)*
>
> *125 g (4 oz) tasty cheese, grated*
>
> *1¼ cups (300 ml/10 fl oz) light sour cream*

Preheat oven to 180°C (350°F).

Wash spinach thoroughly, dry and remove stems. Purée in food processor or electric blender with 1 cup (250 ml/8 fl oz) stock. Pour into large saucepan with remaining stock and add garlic, soup, chillies, cornflour, half the onion, and half the mushrooms. Bring to the boil and set aside.

Combine cottage cheese, olives, chicken and remaining onion and mushrooms. To this, add ½ cup of the spinach mixture and stir until combined. Make tortillas and place 1 heaped tablespoon of chicken mixture in the centre of each tortilla

as soon as it is cooked. Roll up and arrange side by side in a large, greased, shallow ovenproof dish. Pour the spinach sauce over and bake for 20 minutes until bubbly. Sprinkle with cheese and brown under hot grill.

Spread with sour cream and return to the oven for 5 minutes to heat through.

Serve immediately accompanied by a salad.

Note: This dish may be prepared in advance and frozen. Defrost before cooking.

SERVES 6

TORTILLAS

> *1 kg (2 lb) plain (all-purpose) flour*
>
> *2 teaspoons salt*
>
> *250 g (8 oz) butter*
>
> *tepid water*

Sift flour and salt. Cut in butter and mix well, rubbing in with fingertips. Add enough tepid water to form a soft dough. Turn onto a lightly floured board and knead a few times. Divide into 24 balls the size of an egg, cover with a cloth, and let stand for 20 minutes. Roll out balls into flat pancakes or tortillas. Cook in an ungreased frying pan, turning once, until lightly browned on each side. Fill while tortilla is still warm.

MAKES 24

Add enough tepid water to form soft dough.

Cover and let stand for 20 minutes.

Roll out flat pancake shapes or tortillas, cook in ungreased frying pan.

Spinach Chicken Enchiladas

QUICK CHICKEN AND CHEESE CASSEROLE

500 g (1 lb) chopped cooked chicken

370 g (12 oz) cooked rice (150 g (5 oz) raw)

180 g (6 oz) grated tasty cheese

½ cup (125 ml/4 fl oz) milk or cream

1 x 430 g (14 oz) can cream of asparagus soup

1 small onion, finely chopped or grated

60 g (2 oz) butter, melted

35 g (1¼ oz) crushed cornflake crumbs

2 tablespoons oat bran

Preheat oven to 180°C (350°F).

Combine chicken, rice, ½ cup cheese, milk, soup and onion and spoon into a greased 1½ litre (48 fl oz) casserole.

Mix melted butter with cereal, oat bran and remaining cheese and sprinkle over top.

Bake for 30 minutes until top is golden, or microwave on high for 5 to 7 minutes.

Serve hot with peas or beans and warm wholemeal bread rolls.

SERVES 4 TO 6

CHICKEN PIZZA

2 leeks, thinly sliced

2 tablespoons olive oil

2 cups (500 ml/16 fl oz) napolitana or similar tomato based pasta sauce (bottled sauce could be used in this recipe for added convenience)

500 g (1 lb) chopped cooked chicken

2 pre-cooked vacuum packed pizza bases or rounds of focaccia bread

125 g (4 oz) grated mozzarella cheese

2 tablespoons grated Parmesan cheese

chopped olives and anchovies, optional

Preheat oven to 250°C (480°F).

Gently fry leeks in oil until soft. Stir in napolitana sauce and chicken. Heat pizza bases in oven for 5 minutes. Remove and spread each one with half the chicken mixture. Sprinkle mozzarella and Parmesan cheese over the top of each pizza. Top with olives and anchovies if liked. Return to oven and cook for 5 to 10 minutes until piping hot.

To serve, cut pizzas in half and serve on individual dinner plates accompanied by a green salad.

SERVES 4

BUTTERED BREADCRUMBS

Prepare buttered breadcrumbs by sautéing fresh breadcrumbs in a little butter until completely coated.

CHICKEN, CRAB AND AVOCADO

This recipe can be halved to serve 4 people.

2 avocados

1 tablespoon fresh lemon juice

2 tablespoons chopped onion

60 g (2 oz) butter

60 g (2 oz) plain (all-purpose) flour

1 tablespoon shredded fresh mint or basil

¾ teaspoon salt

¾ teaspoon paprika

3 cups (750 ml/24 fl oz) chicken stock

½ cup (125 ml/4 fl oz) light sour cream

750 g (1½ lb) chopped cooked chicken

2 x 170 g (5½ oz) cans crabmeat, drained

1 cup buttered toasted breadcrumbs

Preheat oven to 180°C (350°F).

Peel and seed avocados. Cut into chunks and mix gently with lemon juice. Cook onion gently in butter until golden. Stir in flour, mint, salt and paprika. Cook on a medium heat for 2 minutes stirring continuously. Gradually add stock, stirring constantly. Bring to boil and simmer for 2 minutes. Remove from heat. Gradually blend in sour cream. Add chicken and crabmeat. Pour into 2 litre (64 fl oz) casserole and cover with crumbs. Bake for 30 minutes or microwave on high for 10 minutes. Serve topped with avocado.

Serve with rice and asparagus or green beans.

SERVES 6 TO 8

CHINATOWN CHICKEN

2 tablespoons oil

1 large onion, cut into wedges

1 clove garlic, crushed

2 tablespoons cornflour (cornstarch)

1 cup (250 ml/8 fl oz) orange juice

1 cup (250 ml/8 fl oz) chicken stock

2 tablespoons soy sauce

1 tablespoon brown sugar

1 x 2 cm (¾ in) piece ginger, grated

1 cup snow peas (mangetout)

1 carrot, thinly sliced diagonally

1 x 1.5 kg (3 lb) cooked chicken

Heat oil and gently fry onion and garlic until soft. Stir in cornflour and cook for 1 minute. Gradually add orange juice, stirring constantly. Add stock, soy sauce, brown sugar and ginger and stir until boiling. Add snow peas and carrot and simmer for 5 minutes. Meanwhile, cut chicken into serving portions, discard backbone and wing tips. Add chicken to sauce and heat through.

Serve with rice and snow pea sprouts.

SERVES 4

CHICKEN TETRAZZINI

125 g (4 oz) butter

3 tablespoons plain (all-purpose) flour

2 cups (500 ml/16 fl oz) chicken stock

Tabasco sauce

250 g (8 oz) mushrooms, sliced

½ cup sliced red capsicum (pepper)

½ cup sliced green capsicum (pepper)

1 tablespoon dry sherry

¼ cup (60 ml/2 fl oz) cream

500 g (1 lb) chopped cooked chicken

250 g (8 oz) pasta noodles, cooked

60 g (2 oz) grated Parmesan cheese

Preheat oven to 180°C (350°F).

Melt half the butter in a saucepan. Stir in flour and cook for 1 minute. Gradually add stock and bring to the boil, stirring constantly. Season with a dash of Tabasco sauce.

Cook mushrooms and capsicums gently in remaining butter until soft. Add mushrooms, capsicums, sherry, cream and chicken to sauce.

Arrange alternate layers of the pasta, sauce mixture and generous sprinklings of Parmesan cheese in a greased ovenproof dish. Sprinkle top with Parmesan cheese. Dish can be pre-prepared to this stage and baked when ready to eat. Cover and bake for 30 minutes or until bubbling hot. Brown cheese under grill if liked, before serving.

Serve hot with salad and warm Italian bread.

SERVES 4

MEDITERRANEAN CHICKEN

3 tablespoons olive oil

60 g (2 oz) butter

2 kg (4 lb) chicken cut into serving size pieces

1 onion, finely chopped

2 whole cloves garlic

250 g (8 oz) button mushrooms, thickly sliced

1 tablespoon mixed finely chopped fresh herbs, eg basil, sage, oregano, parsley

salt and freshly ground black pepper

½ cup (125 ml/4 fl oz) white wine

¾ cup (200 ml/6½ fl oz) chicken stock

2 tablespoons plain (all-purpose) flour

¾ cup (200 ml/6½ fl oz) cream

100 g (3 oz) sun-dried tomatoes which have been marinated in olive oil

Heat oil and butter in a deep heatproof casserole. Sauté chicken pieces until brown on all sides. Remove from pan and set to one side.

Add onion and garlic to pan and sauté until golden, about 10 minutes, stirring often.

Add mushrooms and herbs, toss to coat and season with salt and pepper. Discard cloves garlic.

Pour in wine and reduce quickly over a high heat. Stir in stock, bring to the boil then reduce heat.

Blend flour with cream and gradually stir into pan. Cook gently, stirring often until sauce has thickened.

Return chicken to pan and stir in dried tomatoes. Cook over moderate heat for 10 to 15 minutes.

SERVES 4

Salads and Sauces

*T*he chicken salad recipes in this section are the perfect food for long summer days, providing fuss-free, prepare ahead meals that leave you plenty of time to enjoy the season.

Use the sauces to turn a simple meal into something special.

CHICKEN SALAD NICOISE

1 lettuce

250 g (8 oz) green beans, lightly cooked and cooled

½ cup (125 ml/4 fl oz) French dressing

1 Lebanese cucumber, sliced

6 radishes, sliced

500 g (1 lb) chopped cooked chicken

12 cherry tomatoes

2 hard-boiled eggs, cut in quarters

1 x 50 g (1⅔ oz) can anchovy fillets, drained

12 black olives, stoned and halved

125 g (4 oz) shredded mint

Tear lettuce into a salad bowl. Green beans may be steamed and cooled quickly by covering with ¼ cup French dressing.

Sprinkle beans, cucumber and radishes over lettuce. Top with cooked chicken. Scatter cherry tomatoes on top then arrange eggs, anchovy fillets and olives on top.

Mix remaining dressing with mint and pour over salad just before serving.

Toss the salad at the serving table until well coated.

Serve accompanied by tiny new potatoes (chats) and/or garlic bread.

SERVES 4

Dishes on previous pages: Chicken Avocado and Tamarillo Salad (page 55), Chicken and Mango Salad (page 51)

BILPIN APPLE AND CHICKEN SALAD

500 g (1 lb) chopped cooked chicken

125 g (4 oz) chopped red skinned apple

3 tablespoons fresh lemon juice

75 g (2½ oz) chopped black olives

60 g (2 oz) chopped celery

2 tablespoons mayonnaise

2 tablespoons sour cream

salt and pepper

4 lettuce leaves to serve

Mix chicken and apple with lemon juice. Combine remaining ingredients and season to taste with salt and pepper. Add chicken mixture and toss together lightly.

Serve salad in lettuce cups accompanied by a tomato salad and a green salad.

SERVES 4

Bilpin Apple and Chicken Salad

PASTA AND CHICKEN SALAD

300 g (10 oz) cooked macaroni or pasta shells

500 g (1 lb) chopped smoked cooked chicken

100 g (3⅓ oz) blanched broccoli florets

1 teaspoon minced chilli

2 tablespoons thinly sliced spring onions (shallots)

½ cup (125 ml/4 fl oz) mayonnaise

1 tablespoon white wine vinegar

1 clove garlic, crushed

pinch of dry mustard

Combine all ingredients.

Serve salad chilled accompanied by cherry tomato salad and radicchio lettuce.

SERVES 4 TO 6

CHICKEN AND ANCHOVY SALAD

DRESSING

2 egg yolks

1 teaspoon prepared mustard

freshly ground black pepper

¾ cup (180 ml/6 fl oz) olive oil

juice of ½ lemon

2 tablespoons cream

1 small onion, finely diced

1 teaspoon capers

SALAD

2 cups diced cooked chicken

1 mignonette lettuce

1 x 100 g (3⅓ oz) can anchovy fillets

8 stuffed green olives, sliced

To prepare the dressing: Whisk the egg yolks together, add mustard and pepper. Slowly blend in the oil drop by drop until mixture is thick, creamy and even in consistency. A blender may be used, pouring oil from the top. Stir in lemon juice and cream. Finally, add onion and capers.

Toss the diced chicken in the dressing and chill for 30 minutes. Use lettuce to line a salad bowl. Spoon in chicken mixture. Decorate with anchovy fillets placed in criss-cross lattice pattern and top with olives.

Serve salad chilled accompanied by new baby potatoes and a green salad.

SERVES 4

BLANCHING VEGETABLES

Blanch vegetables by immersing in boiling water for 30 seconds to 1 minute to partially cook. Refresh under cold running water.

CHICKEN AND MANGO SALAD

2 cooked chicken breast fillets

1 bunch asparagus

1 large or 2 small mangoes, peeled and sliced

60 g (2 oz) sliced celery

1 cup mixed salad greens or snow pea sprouts

mignonette lettuce leaves

DRESSING

3 tablespoons olive oil

3 tablespoons fresh lime juice

1 clove garlic, crushed

1 teaspoon chopped ginger

1 teaspoon chopped chilli

2 tablespoons shredded coriander or basil

½ teaspoon sugar

The chicken breast fillets may be taken from a barbecued chicken or cooked in a microwave oven on high for 4 minutes.

Cut chicken into strips, pour dressing over, toss lightly until all chicken is coated then allow to stand for 30 minutes to develop flavour. Trim asparagus, cut stems in half, cook lightly and refresh in iced water to preserve bright green colour. Drain well. Fold asparagus, mango and celery into chicken mixture. Add salad greens and lettuce and toss lightly just before serving.

Dressing: Mix all ingredients together in a screw-top jar. Chill until required.

Serve salad immediately accompanied by soft dinner rolls.

SERVES 4

ORIENTAL CHICKEN AND ORANGE SALAD

500g (1 lb) chopped cooked chicken

2 oranges, peeled and segmented

1 stalk celery, sliced diagonally

180 g (6 oz) shredded Chinese cabbage

12 snow peas (mangetout)

6 button mushrooms, sliced

DRESSING

½ cup (125 ml/4 fl oz) fresh orange juice

1 tablespoon light soy sauce

1 teaspoon sesame oil

1 teaspoon finely chopped ginger

1 clove garlic, crushed

1 tablespoon toasted sesame seeds

Place prepared salad ingredients in a salad bowl. Add dressing and toss gently.

Dressing: Mix all ingredients together in a screw-top jar. Chill until required.

Serve salad with a rice salad or bread rolls.

SERVES 4

DIJON CHICKEN AND HAM SALAD

375 g (12 oz) chopped cooked chicken

375 g (12 oz) chopped cooked ham

½ teaspoon grated onion

4 tablespoons French dressing

¾ cup (180 ml/6 fl oz) mayonnaise

2 tablespoons Dijon mustard

1 stick celery, sliced

60 g (2 oz) hazelnuts or pecans, coarsely chopped

1 lettuce

3 tomatoes, sliced

3 hard-boiled eggs, sliced

Combine chicken, ham and onion and marinate for 1 hour in French dressing. Mix mayonnaise with mustard. Mix chicken mixture with mayonnaise mixture, celery and pecans.

Arrange a bed of lettuce on a serving plate, pile chicken mixture in centre and garnish with tomato and egg.

Serve salad with a crisp green salad and garlic bread.

SERVES 4 TO 6

Dijon Chicken and Ham Salad

RICE AND AVOCADO CHICKEN SALAD

220 g (7 oz) long grain rice

500 g (1 lb) cooked chicken meat

2 grapefruits

2 carrots

2 teaspoons finely chopped onion

salt and pepper

1 large ripe avocado

2 tablespoons fresh lemon juice

1 tablespoon vinegar

1 tablespoon olive oil

lettuce or shredded Chinese cabbage

1 cup watercress or snow pea sprouts

DRESSING

½ cup (125 ml/4 fl oz) mayonnaise

1 teaspoon curry powder

Cook rice in sufficient boiling salted water to cover for 10 to 12 minutes, drain thoroughly, rinse in cold water and drain again. Cut chicken into cubes. Peel and segment grapefruit, discarding the pith and membranes. Cut carrots into matchstick-sized strips. Place these prepared ingredients into a bowl with the onion and season to taste with salt and pepper. Toss well.

Peel and dice the avocado and sprinkle with lemon juice. Blend together the vinegar and oil. Add to chicken mixture with avocado and lemon juice. Toss lightly

Serve salad on a bed of lettuce or Chinese cabbage, topped with watercress, accompanied by dressing.

Blend dressing ingredients and place in a small bowl.

Serve with asparagus salad and soft bread rolls.

SERVES 4

TROPICAL CHICKEN SALAD

Tropical Chicken Salad

2 pineapples

1 small pawpaw, peeled, seeded and chopped

2 bananas, chopped

2 kiwifruit, peeled and sliced

8 strawberries, halved

500 g (1 lb) chopped cooked chicken

2 tablespoons pine nuts

mint sprigs

DRESSING

125 ml (4 fl oz) light sour cream

250 g (8 oz) cottage cheese

2 tablespoons shredded mint

Cut pineapples in half, leaving leaves intact. Hollow out the fruit and chop the pineapple. Invert and drain shells and place in refrigerator while preparing other ingredients. Add prepared fruit and chicken to pineapple chunks. Fill pineapple shells with salad.

Dressing: Combine dressing ingredients, spoon over salad. Sprinkle with pine nuts and garnish with mint.

Serve salad accompanied by a rice salad and salad greens if liked, or serve alone for a low kilojoule/low calorie meal.

SERVES 4

CHICKEN AVOCADO AND TAMARILLO SALAD

- 500 g (1 lb) chopped cooked chicken
- ½ cup (125 ml/4 fl oz) French dressing
- 1 small oak leaf lettuce
- 1 small mignonette lettuce
- 60 g (2 oz) sliced fennel
- 1 avocado, peeled, seeded and sliced
- 2 tamarillos, peeled and sliced

Mix chicken with half the dressing and allow to stand for 30 minutes to absorb the flavour.

Tear lettuce into a serving bowl. Add chicken, fennel, avocado, tamarillo and remaining dressing and toss gently until lettuce leaves glisten.

Serve salad immediately with crisp bread rolls.

SERVES 4

AVOCADOS

If leaving sliced avocado exposed to air, brush lightly with lemon juice to help prevent discolouration.

AVOCADO CHICKEN SALAD

- 1 tablespoon oil
- 30 g (1 oz) slivered almonds
- 2 avocados
- juice of 1 lemon
- 1 cucumber, sliced
- 4 chicken breast fillets, skinned cooked and sliced
- 4 stalks celery, sliced
- 1¼ cups (300 ml/10 fl oz) cream
- 2 tablespoons mayonnaise
- 2 tablespoons French dressing
- 1 teaspoon paprika
- ½ teaspoon grated nutmeg
- salt and pepper
- 1 lettuce

Heat oil in a small frying pan and lightly brown almonds; drain on absorbent kitchen paper towels. Halve, stone and peel avocados. Cut into lengthwise slices and coat with lemon juice. Reserve some avocado and cucumber slices to garnish.

Combine chicken, almonds, avocados, cucumber and celery. Whip cream until thick, mix with mayonnaise and French Dressing and season with paprika and nutmeg. Pour over chicken mixture and toss gently.

Spoon mixture into lettuce leaves, garnish with remaining avocado slices and cucumber slices.

Serve with a green salad and a pasta salad.

SERVES 4

TEXAN CHICKEN SALAD

- juice of 1 lemon
- 2 avocados, peeled, seeded and sliced
- 1 kg (2 lb) chopped cooked chicken
- 1 red capsicum (pepper) or sweet chilli pepper, sliced
- 125 g (4 oz) sultana grapes
- 60 g (2 oz) chopped pecans or walnuts
- 6 to 7 tablespoons mayonnaise
- 1 lettuce

Pour lemon juice over avocado slices. Mix together chicken, capsicum, grapes, pecans and mayonnaise. Arrange avocado slices on lettuce and spoon chicken mixture on top.

Serve salad with a rice salad.

SERVES 8

TZADZIKI SAUCE

- 1 x 200 g (6½ oz) carton natural yoghurt
- 250 g (8 oz) cottage cheese
- 2 cloves garlic, crushed
- 2 tablespoons shredded mint
- ½ cup peeled, seeded and thinly sliced cucumber

Mix yoghurt, cottage cheese and garlic together in a blender or food processor.

Fold in the mint and cucumber. Cover and chill before serving.

Serve as a dipping sauce with Chicken Burghul Balls.

MAKES 2 CUPS (500 ML/16 FL OZ)

Chicken Avocado and Tamarillo Salad

Sauce Bigarrade, Cold Ravigote Sauce,
Mustard Cream Sauce

SAUCE BIGARRADE

*2 bitter oranges or 1 orange and
½ lemon*

*1 x 410 g (13 oz) can beef
consommé*

*½ cup (125 ml/4 fl oz) white
wine*

2 tablespoons Madeira or port

drippings from pan, fat removed

Carefully peel rind from fruit and
cut into thin julienne strips. Pour
boiling water over to cover. Let
stand for 5 minutes and then drain
and set rind aside.

Squeeze juice from oranges, strain
and mix with beef consommé, wine
and Madeira. Bring to boil and
simmer for 5 minutes to reduce
liquid and concentrate flavour.

When poultry has been removed
from roasting pan, skim off all fat
from drippings. Combine pan
drippings and sediment with orange
and wine mixture and simmer,
stirring until sauce is smooth and
well blended. Stir in citrus rind.

Serve sauce hot with roast chicken or
duck.

**MAKES 1½ CUPS
(375 ML/12 FL OZ)**

PAN SEDIMENT

Sediment is what is left behind when you
remove baked meat from the pan.
It provides a flavoursome base for sauces
and gravies. In a traditional gravy it is
mixed with flour to add thickness.
Here it is combined with citrus juices to
make an unusual, thinner sauce
to go with roast chicken.

COLD RAVIGOTE
SAUCE

*1 cup chopped mixed fresh herbs
(parsley, tarragon, mint,
chervil, watercress, chives)*

1 cup (250 ml/8 fl oz) olive oil

*4 tablespoons tarragon flavoured
white wine vinegar*

1 tablespoon capers, chopped

Combine all ingredients thoroughly
and chill.

Cook 8 chicken breast fillets by
steaming or in a microwave oven,
then pour ravigote sauce over while
still hot. Allow to cool so that
chicken may absorb flavour of sauce.
Serve chicken breasts cold
accompanied by mixed salads or
chop and use in a chicken salad.

**MAKES 1½ CUPS
(375 ML/12 FL OZ)**

MUSTARD
CREAM SAUCE

½ cup (125 ml/4 fl oz) water

sediment from 1 roast chicken

*1 tablespoon dried onion flakes,
optional*

*1 tablespoon French wholegrain
mustard*

1 tablespoon tomato sauce

2 teaspoons Worcestershire sauce

*1 cup (250 ml/8 fl oz) light sour
cream*

salt and pepper

Add water to sediment in baking
dish/roasting tin and bring to the
boil. Add onion flakes, mustard and
sauces and simmer for 5 minutes.
Strain into a saucepan and stir in
sour cream and salt and pepper to
taste.

Serve sauce hot with roast chicken.

**MAKES 1½ CUPS
(435 ML/14 FL OZ)**

CRANBERRY RELISH

*1 x 300 g (10 oz) jar cranberry
    sauce*

*75 g (2½ oz) chopped dried
    apricots*

40 g (1½ oz) sultanas

¼ cup (60 ml/2 fl oz) water

1 teaspoon grated orange rind

¼ teaspoon ground ginger

1 tablespoon brown sugar

Combine cranberry sauce, apricots, sultanas, water, orange rind and ginger in a saucepan. Bring to the boil and simmer 10 minutes. Add sugar and cook for 1 minute or until dissolved. Cool. Pour into sterilised jars and seal. Store in refrigerator. Use within one week of making.

Serve with hot or cold roast chicken, smoked chicken or turkey.

**MAKES 2 CUPS
(500 ML/16 FL OZ)**

BREAD SAUCE

1 onion, chopped

2 cloves

½ cup (125 ml/4 fl oz) cream

*1½ cups (375 ml/12 fl oz)
    chicken stock*

60 g (2 oz) fresh breadcrumbs

freshly ground black pepper

Add onion and cloves to cream and stock in a saucepan, cover and simmer 15 minutes. Whisk in crumbs with a fork and continue to cook over a very low heat for 10 minutes, stirring occasionally until sauce thickens. Season to taste with pepper.

Serve sauce hot with roast chicken.

**MAKES 2 CUPS
(500 ML/16 FL OZ)**

PROVENCALE SAUCE

1 tablespoon olive oil

1 onion, finely chopped

2 cloves garlic, crushed

1 x 410 g (13 oz) can tomatoes

*1 cup (250 ml/8 fl oz) chicken or
    vegetable stock*

*1 tablespoon chopped fresh
    parsley*

1 tablespoon shredded fresh basil

Heat oil and gently fry onion and garlic until soft and golden, stirring frequently. Add remaining ingredients and simmer until sauce has a thick consistency.

Serve sauce with cooked/barbecued chicken, rice and salad or a green vegetable.

SERVES 4

*Cranberry Relish, Bread Sauce,
Provençale Sauce*

Light and Easy Meals

*T*he light and easy recipes using chicken pieces in this section will give you ideas for a variety of simple meals. Most of them can be prepared, cooked and served within 30 minutes.

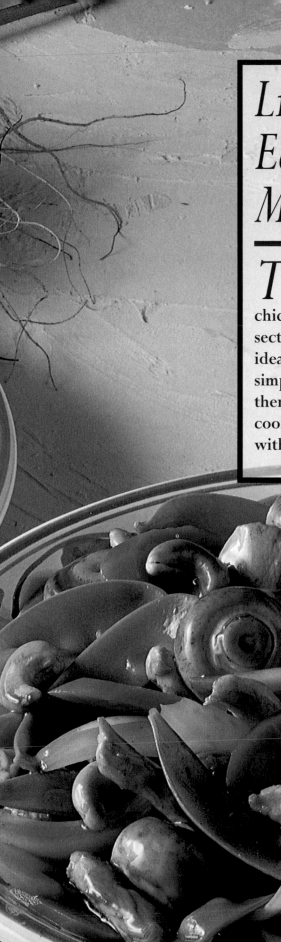

CHICKEN DIANE

4 chicken breast fillets, skinned

freshly ground black pepper

60 g (2 oz) butter

2 cloves garlic, crushed

2 tablespoons Worcestershire sauce

2 tablespoons brandy

2 tablespoons cream

2 tablespoons finely chopped fresh parsley

Season chicken lightly with pepper. Melt butter in a sauté or frying pan, add garlic.

When sizzling, add chicken breasts and cook for 2 minutes on each side. Add Worcestershire sauce, cover pan and simmer chicken over a medium heat for 12 minutes, turning after 6 minutes.

Warm brandy in a small saucepan for 15 to 20 seconds, flame it then pour over the chicken. Stir in cream and parsley.

Serve Chicken Diane with new baby potatoes (chats) or rice and asparagus.

SERVES 4

CHICKEN SAUTE WITH DILL AND MUSHROOMS

Dill may be replaced with any seasonal herb such as basil, parsley or oregano.

4 chicken breast fillets, skinned

2 white onions, thinly sliced

60 g (2 oz) butter

125 g (4 oz) mushroom buttons or cups, sliced

⅓ cup (80 ml/2⅔ fl oz) dry white wine

⅓ cup (80 ml/2⅔ fl oz) chicken stock

⅓ cup (80 ml/2⅔ fl oz) cream

2 tablespoons shredded fresh dill or tarragon

Trim chicken breasts neatly. Gently fry onions in butter in a sauté pan or a large frying pan until soft. Add chicken breasts and fry on both sides until colour changes. Add mushrooms and fry for 1 minute. Add wine and stock and bring to the boil, then simmer, covered, for 10 minutes or until chicken is cooked. Stir in cream and dill and heat through gently.

Serve chicken sauté with lemon rice and a green vegetable.

SERVES 4

CHICKEN CUTS

Chicken thigh fillets are a good alternative to chicken breast fillets and often have a tastier flavour, so experiment with some different cuts.

CAMEMBERT STUFFED POUSSIN

This is an impressive chicken dish to serve when entertaining.

4 dressed poussin or spatchcock

2 x 125 g (4 oz) rounds of camembert cheese

2 tablespoons olive oil

30 g (1 oz) butter, melted

freshly ground black pepper

Preheat oven to 220°C (440°F).

Rinse cavities of poussins with cold water and wipe poussins with a clean damp cloth. Cut cheeses in half and place half a camembert round in the cavity of each poussin. Truss by tying legs together with white kitchen string and pull neck skin back and secure with wings. Place on a rack in a baking dish/roasting tin, brush with olive oil mixed with melted butter and sprinkle with black pepper. Roast in an oven for 45 to 60 minutes, basting occasionally, until golden brown and cooked.

Serve poussin accompanied by a wild rice risotto and creamed spinach.

SERVES 4

STUFFED ZUCCHINI (COURGETTES)

16 small zucchini (courgettes)

250 g (8 oz) chopped cooked chicken

100 g (3⅓ oz) continental sausage, mortadella or salami

1 egg

2 tablespoons dry breadcrumbs

¼ cup (60 ml/2 fl oz) milk

2 tablespoons grated Parmesan cheese

salt

Dishes on previous pages: Chicken Sauté with Dill and Mushrooms (page 60), Stir Fry Chicken and Cashews (page 66)

Stuffed Zucchini (Courgettes)

Carefully remove centre of each zucchini with apple corer.

Mince stuffing ingredients in food processor or blender.

Using a piping bag with a plain nozzle, pipe stuffing into zucchini.

freshly ground black pepper

grated nutmeg

2 tablespoons olive oil

40 g (1⅓ oz) butter

1 large onion, finely chopped

½ cup (125 ml/4 fl oz) white wine

3 tomatoes, finely chopped

Remove centre of zucchini with an apple corer. Mix chicken, sausage, egg, breadcrumbs, milk and cheese together and mince in a food processor or electric blender.

Season to taste with salt, pepper and nutmeg. Spoon into a piping bag with a plain nozzle and pipe into zucchini.

Heat oil and butter in a pan, add onion and cook until golden brown. Add zucchini and cook a further 5 minutes. Add wine, cover and simmer for 10 minutes. Add tomatoes, cover and simmer gently for 20 minutes.

Serve Stuffed Zucchini with rice.

SERVES 8 FOR AN ENTREE, SERVES 4 FOR A MAIN COURSE

CHICKEN ROLLS WITH PRAWN (SHRIMP) SAUCE

250 g (8 oz) smoked cod

4 cloves garlic

1 tablespoon chopped chives

1 teaspoon fennel seeds

4 chicken breast fillets, skinned

freshly ground black pepper

2 tablespoons olive oil

20 g (⅔ oz) butter

1 tablespoon plain (all-purpose) flour

¼ cup (60 ml/2 fl oz) white wine

2 teaspoons fresh lemon juice

100 g (3⅓ oz) button mushrooms, sliced

1 x 100 g (3⅓ oz) can peeled prawns (shrimp), drained

½ cup (125 ml/4 fl oz) cream

Preheat oven to 190°C (375°F).

Purée cod, garlic, chives and fennel seeds in food processor or electric blender. Flatten chicken with a cleaver or rolling pin. Sprinkle with pepper. Divide fish mixture between chicken breasts and roll up. Arrange in a greased shallow ovenproof dish, overlapping side down. Brush with oil, sprinkle with pepper, cover and bake for 20 to 30 minutes until

tender. Pour off pan juices and reserve. Keep chicken warm.

Melt butter in a saucepan, stir in flour and cook 1 minute. Gradually stir in reserved chicken juices, wine and lemon juice and simmer for 2 to 3 minutes. Add mushrooms and cook a further 3 to 4 minutes until tender. Stir in prawns and cream and season to taste with pepper.

Chicken and Prawn (Shrimp) Soufflé

Serve chicken rolls sliced, coated with prawn sauce, accompanied with pasta noodles and brussel sprouts sprinkled with toasted sesame seeds.

SERVES 4

SOUFFLE DISHES

Take a strip of foil and fold to form one long, thin piece. Grease one side of the foil. Tie the foil around the top of the soufflé dish with string. This 'collar' will keep the soufflé's height as it rises. Remove before serving.

CHICKEN AND PRAWN (SHRIMP) SOUFFLE

1 chicken breast fillet, cooked

100 g (3⅓ oz) can peeled prawns (shrimps), drained

3 tablespoons chicken stock

60 g (2 oz) butter

3 tablespoons plain (all-purpose) flour

150 ml (5 fl oz) milk

salt and pepper

6 eggs, separated

2 egg whites

2 tablespoons dry breadcrumbs

Preheat oven to 180°C (350°F).

The chicken fillet may be poached gently or cooked in a microwave oven with sufficient water and wine to cover. Purée chicken, prawns and stock in a food processor or electric blender. Set aside.

Melt butter in a saucepan, stir in flour and cook 1 minute. Gradually add milk, stirring constantly and cook until thickened. (The sauce should be very thick.) Stir in chicken purée, season with salt and pepper and cool. Blend in egg yolks.

Whisk egg whites until stiff and fold half into the chicken mixture. Lightly fold in remaining half. Butter 6 individual soufflé dishes, or one large soufflé dish, and sprinkle sides with breadcrumbs. Pour mixture into dishes and bake for 20 minutes (35 minutes if using larger dish).

Serve immediately accompanied by garlic bread and salad.

Note: This dish can be prepared in advance to the point of whisking the egg whites. Sauce can be made in a microwave oven. Make sure your guests are ready to eat this impressive Chicken and Prawn Soufflé the minute it comes out of the oven.

SERVES 6

CHICKEN WITH CURRIED MARMALADE SAUCE

60 g (2 oz) butter

4 chicken tenderloin fillets

1 tablespoon plain (all-purpose) flour

1 tablespoon curry powder or paste

2 tablespoons sherry

4 tablespoons orange marmalade

½ cup (125 ml/4 fl oz) orange juice

Heat butter in a frying pan, add chicken and fry gently for 5 minutes or until tender. Remove chicken and set aside.

Add flour and curry powder and stir fry for 1 minute. Add sherry, marmalade and orange juice. Stir until marmalade melts. Return chicken to pan and heat through.

Serve hot with fried potato balls or rice and snow peas or green beans.

SERVES 2

CHICKEN MOLE

- 500 g (1 lb) boneless chicken thighs
- 1 onion, sliced
- 1 clove garlic, crushed
- 1 cup (250 ml/8 fl oz) chicken stock

MOLE SAUCE

- 1 x 425 g (14 oz) can tomatoes, drained
- 1 banana, peeled and sliced
- 2 corn tortillas, torn in pieces or 2 slices toast
- 40 g (1½ oz) blanched almonds
- 1 tablespoon chilli powder
- ½ teaspoon ground cinnamon
- ¼ teaspoon ground cloves
- 125 g (4 oz) butter
- 60 g (2 oz) unsweetened chocolate
- 2 tablespoons chopped fresh coriander (cilantro) leaves
- 1 tablespoon sesame seeds

Place chicken pieces in a pan with onion and garlic, cover with stock and simmer for 20 to 30 minutes or until tender. Remove and allow to cool. Strain and reserve stock.

Purée tomatoes, banana, tortillas and almonds with spices in a food processor or electric blender. Gradually add stock until sauce is consistency of pouring cream. Pour sauce into a saucepan, add butter and chocolate and heat until chocolate is melted. Add more chicken stock if necessary.

Add chicken and simmer until heated through.

Serve Chicken Mole on a bed of rice and garnish with coriander and sesame seeds. Accompany with a refreshing salad.

SERVES 4

CREAMY VINDALOO CHICKEN

- 4 chicken breast fillets, skinned
- 30 g (1 oz) butter
- 1 onion, chopped
- 4 tablespoons vindaloo curry paste
- 1 cup (250 ml/8 fl oz) chicken stock or water
- 2 tablespoons tomato paste
- ½ cup (125 ml/4 fl oz) cream

Trim chicken breasts of excess fat and cartilage. Heat butter in a large frying pan and gently fry onion until soft, about 5 minutes, push to side of pan. Add chicken breasts and fry on both sides until colour changes. Add curry paste and stir-fry for 1 minute. Add stock and tomato paste, bring to the boil, cover and simmer for 5 to 10 minutes until chicken is cooked. Stir in cream and heat through gently.

Serve with rice and curry accompaniments such as diced tomato and cucumber in oil and vinegar dressing and sliced banana and shredded coconut in natural yoghurt and pappadums.

SERVES 4

CHICKEN STOCK

Place chicken bones and giblets in a large saucepan with roughly chopped onions, carrots and celery. Add a bouquet garni, peppercorns and enough water to cover. Bring to the boil. Reduce heat. Simmer for about 3 hours. Skim scum off surface. When cool, remove fat from surface then strain. Refrigerate or freeze.

GREEN CURRIED CHICKEN

Green curry paste and kaffir lime leaves are available in leading Asian food stores.

- 500 g (1 lb) chicken breast fillets, skinned
- 1 tablespoon peanut or safflower oil
- 2 tablespoons green curry paste
- 1 teaspoon chopped ginger
- 1 x 410 g (13 fl oz) coconut milk
- 1 cup (250 ml/8 fl oz) water
- 4 dried kaffir lime leaves
- 1 tablespoon fish sauce
- 1 coriander (cilantro) plant, roots, stems and leaves, chopped
- 1 cup frozen peas, thawed

Trim chicken breasts and cut into strips or 2½ cm (1 in) cubes. Heat oil in a pan, add chicken and stir-fry until colour changes. Add curry paste and ginger and stir-fry for 1 minute. Add all remaining ingredients and bring to the boil then simmer for 10 minutes until chicken is tender.

Serve Green Curried Chicken with rice.

SERVES 4

Chicken Mole

STIR FRY CHICKEN AND CASHEWS

Three cups of any mixed coloured and textured vegetables may be used in this stir-fry recipe as an alternative to those suggested here.

2 large chicken breast fillets, skinned

3 tablespoons peanut oil

1 onion cut into 12 wedges

1 clove garlic, crushed

1 teaspoon chopped ginger

3 sticks diagonally sliced celery

20 snow peas (mangetout)

1 carrot, diagonally sliced

60 g (2 oz) button mushrooms

1 cup (250 ml/8 fl oz) chicken stock

2 tablespoons oyster sauce

2 tablespoons soy sauce

1 tablespoon cornflour (cornstarch)

2 tablespoons mirin or sherry

60 g (2 oz) toasted cashew nuts

Cut chicken breasts into thin strips and stir fry them in oil in a wok or large frying pan for 3 minutes. Add onion, garlic and ginger, stir fry for 1 minute. Add celery, snow peas, carrot and mushrooms and cook another 2 to 3 minutes. Stir in chicken stock, cover and simmer for 5 minutes.

Blend oyster and soy sauces with cornflour and mirin and stir into the mixture until it thickens. Stir in cashews.

Serve with rice or Chinese noodles.

SERVES 4

TASTY THAI DIET CHICKEN

4 chicken breast fillets, skinned

freshly ground black pepper

2 tablespoons peanut or safflower oil

1 clove garlic, crushed

1 teaspoon chopped chilli

1 teaspoon chopped ginger

1 stalk lemongrass, sliced

2 tablespoons light soy sauce

½ cup (125 ml/4 fl oz) chicken stock

2 tablespoons fresh lime juice

2 tablespoons chopped coriander (cilantro) leaves

Cut chicken into long strips. Sprinkle with pepper. Heat oil in a wok or large frying pan and stir-fry until golden.

Add garlic, chilli, ginger and lemongrass and stir-fry for 1 minute. Add remaining ingredients, bring to the boil and simmer for 2 minutes until chicken is tender and moist.

Serve with a green salad.

SERVES 4

Left: Stir Fry Chicken and Cashews
Right: Tasty Thai Diet Chicken

CHICKEN NACHOS

1 large onion, chopped

1 tablespoon olive oil

250 g (8 oz) chicken mince

1 cup (250 ml/8 fl oz) taco sauce

1 x 310 g (10 oz) can red kidney beans, drained

125 g (4 oz) cheddar cheese, grated

1 x 200 g (approximately 7 oz) packet corn chips

sour cream and/or guacamole for serving

Preheat oven to 180°C (350°F).

Gently fry onion in heated oil until soft and transparent. Add chicken mince and stir over heat until colour changes. Add taco sauce and bring to the boil, stirring. Place mixture in a shallow ovenproof baking dish and stir in the beans. Sprinkle half the grated cheese over the top. Cover with corn chips and sprinkle remaining cheese on top.

Bake for 20 to 30 minutes until bubbling hot. To save time, place in a microwave safe dish and cook in a microwave oven on high setting for 8 to 10 minutes until hot.

Serve Chicken Nachos topped with sour cream or guacamole accompanied with a tossed salad.

SERVES 4

CHICKEN LIVERS VERONIQUE

750 g (1½ lb) chicken livers

2 tablespoons seasoned, plain (all purpose) flour

2 tablespoons chopped spring onions (shallots)

60 g (2 oz) butter

3 tablespoons white wine

3 tablespoons chicken stock

185 g (6 oz) seedless grapes

6 tablespoons light sour cream

finely chopped parsley to garnish.

Trim and rinse chicken livers, pat dry and coat with seasoned flour. Gently fry livers and spring onions in butter over a medium heat for 6 to 8 minutes. Pour in wine and stock and bring to the boil. Then add grapes and reduce the heat, cover and cook for 3 minutes. Stir in sour cream and reheat gently.

Serve hot sprinkled with finely chopped parsley accompanied by rice and a green vegetable or salad.

SERVES 6

ONIONS

Onions should be peeled for every recipe, unless otherwise stated. Peel using a sharp knife. If the onion is cold you may cry less while chopping it.

CHICKEN LIVER RISOTTO

1 tablespoon olive oil

1 onion, finely chopped

220 g (7 oz) long grain rice

1 clove garlic, crushed

2 cups (500 ml/16 fl oz) chicken stock

250 g (8 oz) chicken livers, cleaned and roughly chopped

2 rashers bacon, chopped

30 g (1 oz) butter

125 g (4 oz) thawed frozen peas

2 tablespoons chopped fresh parsley

Heat oil in a pan and cook onion until transparent. Add rice and garlic and cook, stirring, until rice is coated with oil. Add stock, stir well, cover and cook over a low heat for 20 minutes or until almost all the liquid is absorbed. The rice should be soft. Add more stock during cooking if necessary.

Cook chicken livers and bacon gently in butter for 5 to 7 minutes until just cooked. Stir with peas into rice and heat through.

Serve risotto hot sprinkled with chopped parsley accompanied by a green salad.

SERVES 4

CRUSHED GARLIC

Crush garlic cloves by chopping finely and then pressing with the blade of a knife to crush. A little salt sprinkled onto the clove before crushing will absorb any garlic juice that escapes. Alternatively, use a garlic press.

FETTUCINE
WITH CHICKEN

400 g (13 oz) spinach fettucine noodles

80 g (2⅔ oz) butter

2 chicken breast fillets, skinned and cut into strips

100 g (3⅓ oz) prosciutto ham, thinly sliced

1¼ cups (300 ml/10 fl oz) cream

½ cup (125 ml/4 fl oz) chicken stock

60 g (2 oz) grated Parmesan cheese

salt

freshly ground black pepper

extra grated Parmesan cheese to serve

Cook noodles in boiling salted water for 10 to 12 minutes until tender. Drain.

Meanwhile heat butter and fry chicken gently for 3 minutes. Add ham, cream, chicken stock and cheese and season to taste with salt and pepper. Cook over a low heat, stirring constantly, until sauce boils. Add to noodles and toss well.

Serve hot with extra grated Parmesan cheese for sprinkling, accompanied with a green salad.

SERVES 4

HEALTHY CHICKEN

Remove skin from chicken pieces to reduce fat, cholesterol and kilojoules. Skin is easily removed from chicken pieces. Simply ease fingertips under skin and pull.

YOGHURT
CHICKEN PAPRIKA

60 g (2 oz) butter

1 onion, chopped

4 chicken breast fillets, skinned

1 tablespoon paprika

1 tablespoon plain (all-purpose) flour

1½ cups (375 ml/12 fl oz) chicken stock

½ green capsicum (pepper), chopped

200 g (6½ oz) carton natural yoghurt

chopped parsley for garnish

Heat butter in a frying or sauté pan and gently fry onion until soft, push to edge of pan. Add chicken breasts and fry on both sides until colour changes. Add paprika and simmer gently for 5 minutes. Add flour and stir over heat for 1 minute. Add stock and capsicum and bring to the boil stirring, then simmer for 5 minutes or until chicken is cooked. Stir in yoghurt and heat through gently.

Serve hot sprinkled with chopped parsley accompanied by pasta noodles or rice and peas or coleslaw salad.

SERVES 4

NON-STICK PANS

Use non-stick pans where possible as it cuts down the need for fat in your chicken dishes.

CHICKEN WITH
LEMON AND
GRAPE SAUCE

30 g (1 oz) butter

4 chicken tenderloin fillets

1 onion, finely chopped

5 thinly sliced spring onions (shallots)

¼ cup (60 ml/2 fl oz) fresh lemon juice

½ cup (125 ml/4 fl oz) chicken stock

1 teaspoon cornflour (cornstarch)

1 tablespoon water

1 cup sultana grapes, halved

julienne of lemon rind

Heat butter in a frying pan until foaming. Add chicken fillets and cook until just brown. Remove and set aside. Add onion and spring onions to pan and fry gently for 1 minute, stirring constantly. Return chicken to pan, add lemon juice and stock, cover and simmer for 5 to 10 minutes until tender. Blend cornflour with 1 tablespoon water, add to pan and stir until sauce thickens. Add grapes and allow to heat through.

Serve hot sprinkled with julienne of lemon rind accompanied with rice and salad.

SERVES 2

Country Chicken

*C*lassical and hearty, traditional country chicken dishes maintain their popularity just as they maintain their flavour. This section offers recipes for favourite roasts, pies and casseroles to make any family gathering a success.

VINTAGE CHICKEN WITH ONIONS

12 chicken pieces (on the bone)

¾ cup (180 ml/6 fl oz) white wine

¼ cup (60 ml/2 fl oz) olive oil

1 bay leaf

½ teaspoon salt

2 cloves garlic, crushed

30 g (1 oz) seasoned flour

60 g (2 oz) butter

2 onions, sliced

1¼ cups (310 ml/10 fl oz) chicken stock

pepper

6 small pickling onions, peeled

extra 30 g (1 oz) butter

125 g (4 oz) button mushrooms

1 kg (2 lb) cooked rice to serve (440 g (14 oz) raw)

Trim excess fat and skin from chicken pieces. Mix wine, oil, bay leaf, salt and garlic and marinate chicken in mixture for at least 2 hours.

Preheat oven to 180°C (350°F).

Drain and toss in seasoned flour. Cook in butter until browned. Arrange in casserole. Cook sliced onions in same pan until browned and add to chicken. Stir remaining marinade and stock into pan sediments and bring to the boil. Season to taste with pepper and pour over chicken. Cover and cook for 30 minutes.

Fry small onions gently in extra butter and add to casserole with mushrooms. Cook for a further 30 minutes. Serve Vintage Chicken with Onions with cooked rice and asparagus or green beans.

SERVES 6

Dishes on previous pages: Chicken and Mushroom Pie (page 77), Riverland Chicken (page 80)

PICKLING ONIONS

Pickling onions are baby onions often available at your greengrocer. If unavailable, use small onions or halve or quarter larger ones.

STEAMED/BAKED BOILER

A boiler may be a tough bird but is economical and has a good flavour.

To steam: Half fill a large pan with cold water. Add 1 peeled, halved onion, 1 bay leaf, ½ teaspoon salt, 6 peppercorns, 1 carrot, halved and 2 stalks celery, sliced. Place the boiler in a steamer over the pan. Cover and bring to the boil, then simmer until chicken is cooked and tender. Clear juice will spurt out when skewered through the thickest part of a leg. If juice is pink, steam longer until juice is clear. Approximate time is 1½ hours. Use stock in a soup or sauce or casserole. This method can be speeded by cooking the boiler in a pressure cooker, half filled with water and the vegetables and seasonings. Approximate time is 30 minutes.

To bake: Sprinkle the boiler with salt, pepper and the juice of 1 lemon. Place 2 rashers bacon over the breast and wrap the bird up in foil. Place on a rack in a baking dish/roasting tin half full of water. Cook in an oven at 160°C (325°F) until tender, approximately 1½ hours.

Use the boiler's meat for recipes that require chopped cooked chicken.

CHICKEN AND PRAWN PAELLA

6 chicken breast fillets, skinned

¼ cup (60 ml/2 fl oz) olive oil

2 onions, chopped

2 cloves garlic, crushed

125 g (4 oz) minced pork

2 tomatoes, peeled and chopped

300 g (10 oz) packet frozen peas, thawed

1 x 320 g (11 oz) can artichoke hearts, drained and halved

2 teaspoons paprika

330 g (10½ oz) long grain rice

1 teaspoon salt

4 cups (1 litre/32 fl oz) chicken stock

1 packet saffron threads soaked in 3 tablespoons boiling water

500 g (1 lb) green prawns, peeled and deveined

16 mussels, scrubbed

16 black olives

Cut chicken into chunky pieces. Heat oil in a paella pan or large frying pan and cook chicken, onion and garlic until brown. Add pork and brown quickly. Add tomatoes, peas, artichokes, paprika and rice. Cook, stirring until rice is well coated with oil. Add salt, stock and saffron, bring to the boil then cover and cook for 15 minutes or until rice is almost tender. Add prawns and mussels and continue cooking until prawns turn pink and mussels open. Sprinkle with olives

Serve paella from pan accompanied by warm French bread and green salad.

Note: If preparing in advance, do not add prawns and mussels until just before serving as they may toughen.

SERVES 8

COUNTRY KITCHEN BOILER

1 x 1.75 kg (3½ lb) boiling fowl

juice and rind of 1 lemon

1 large onion, sliced

1 teaspoon salt

6 peppercorns

2 tablespoons oil

1 chopped onion (extra)

3 sticks celery, chopped

1 to 2 teaspoons chilli powder

1 teaspoon sugar

3 tablespoons tomato paste

freshly ground black pepper

2 teaspoons grated ginger

2 to 3 teaspoons cornflour (cornstarch)

Cut fowl into 12 pieces. Remove all remains of innards. Put in a large pan and barely cover with warm water. Add lemon juice and rind, sliced onion, salt and peppercorns. Bring to the boil and simmer gently for 30 minutes.

Remove fowl with a slotted spoon and set aside. Boil stock rapidly until reduced to 2 cups (500 ml/16 fl oz). Strain and set aside.

Heat oil, gently cook chopped onion until lightly coloured, add celery, reserved stock, chilli powder, sugar, tomato paste, pepper and ginger. Simmer for a few minutes. Add fowl, cover and simmer for 1 hour or until fowl is tender (time depends on age of bird). Blend cornflour with 1 tablespoon cold water, stir into stock and return to the boil, stirring continuously.

Serve with jacket baked potatoes and braised cabbage.

SERVES 6

ITALIAN-STYLE CHICKEN

12 pieces chicken (on the bone)

2 tablespoons seasoned flour

3 tablespoons olive oil

1 onion, finely chopped

1 clove garlic, crushed

2 tomatoes, peeled and chopped

1 green capsicum (pepper), seeded and cut into strips

1 teaspoon mixed dried herbs or 1 tablespoon chopped fresh herbs

1 tablespoon chopped fresh parsley

2 cups (500 ml/16 fl oz) dry red wine

125 g (4 oz) sliced mushrooms

Coat chicken in seasoned flour. Heat oil in large sauté or frying pan, add onion and garlic and cook until soft and golden. Add chicken and brown all over. Cover and cook over low heat for 10 minutes. Add tomatoes, capsicum, herbs and wine. Cover and simmer for 45 minutes. Add mushrooms and cook further 10 minutes until chicken is tender.

Serve hot with pasta and peas or squash.

SERVES 6

PEELING TOMATOES

Peel tomatoes by piercing the skin in a few places. Cover with boiling water. Leave for 1 minute. Drain well. The skin will peel away easily.

TUSCAN CHICKEN

2 x 1.4 kg (2 lb 13 oz) chickens

¼ cup (60 ml/2 fl oz) olive oil

1 cup (250 ml/8 fl oz) dry white wine

1½ cups (375 ml/12 fl oz) vegetable stock

3 tablespoons tomato paste

2 teaspoons dried sage

1 tablespoon capers

4 spring onions, finely chopped

4 celery sticks, sliced

8 green button squash

2 tablespoons chopped parsley

Cut each chicken into eight pieces and trim away the excess fat. Heat the oil in a large heavy-based pan and brown the chicken pieces in batches. Place the pieces in a large baking dish.

Preheat the oven to 180°C (350°F). Combine the wine, stock, tomato paste, sage, capers, spring onions and celery in a medium pan. Stir over medium heat until the mixture boils. Pour over the chicken pieces, cover with aluminium foil and bake for 1 hour.

Add the squash and parsley to the dish. Baste the chicken and squash and return the dish to the oven. Bake, uncovered, for 30 minutes, basting every 10 minutes.

Remove the chicken and squash to a serving dish and keep warm. Pour the cooking juices into a pan. Stir over medium heat until the mixture boils; reduce the heat and simmer for 5 minutes, or until reduced by half. Serve the chicken with the sauce and a green salad.

SERVES 8

Using a teaspoon, spoon mixture into boned legs.

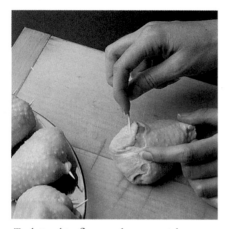

Tuck in skin flaps and secure with toothpicks.

Brown chicken in butter.

ALMOND-STUFFED DRUMSTICKS

125 g (4 oz) almonds, roasted and chopped

60 g (2 oz) butter

125 g (4 oz) chicken livers, cleaned and chopped

1 onion, finely chopped

1 clove garlic, crushed

12 sage leaves or 1 teaspoon dried sage

½ teaspoon dried mixed herbs

salt

freshly ground black pepper

6 large chicken drumsticks, boned

1 cup (250 ml/8 fl oz) white wine

1 tablespoon tomato paste

To roast almonds, spread on a baking tray and bake at 150°C (300°F) for 10 minutes or until a light straw colour. Chop in a food processor or blender.

Heat half the butter in a frying pan. Add livers, onion, garlic and herbs, and cook gently for 5 minutes, stirring. Add half the almonds, season to taste with salt and pepper and cool slightly. Using a teaspoon, spoon mixture into boned legs to stuff. Tuck in skin flaps and secure with toothpicks or sew up if necessary. Brown chicken in remaining butter. Pour wine over, add tomato paste, cover and simmer gently or bake for 45 minutes until tender.

Serve hot sprinkled with remaining almonds, accompanied by sauté potatoes and sauerkraut.

SERVES 6

ORANGE PECAN CHICKEN

1 large orange

60 g (2 oz) butter

1 onion, grated

60 g (2 oz) finely chopped celery

185 g (6 oz) fresh breadcrumbs

60 g (2 oz) chopped pecans

2 tablespoons chopped fresh parsley

½ teaspoon salt

freshly ground black pepper

¼ teaspoon dried thyme

1 x 1.5 kg (3 lb) dressed chicken

Preheat oven to 180°C (350°F).

Grate orange rind and reserve. Remove orange peel and pith using a serrated knife and cut orange into segments.

Melt butter in a small pan. Add onion and celery and cook until soft. Add orange rind and segments, breadcrumbs, pecans, parsley, salt, pepper and thyme and mix well. Spoon mixture into chicken cavity. Truss. Bake for 1 to 1¼ hours or until tender.

Serve chicken cut into four portions accompanied by stuffing, new potatoes and zucchini (courgettes).

SERVES 4

Orange Pecan Chicken

CHICKEN LOAF WITH MUSHROOM SAUCE

- 500 g (1 lb) chicken mince
- 60 g (2 oz) fresh wholegrain breadcrumbs
- ½ green capsicum (pepper), finely chopped
- 2 sticks celery, finely chopped
- 1 onion, finely chopped
- 1 tablespoon fresh lemon juice
- 1 tablespoon Worcestershire sauce
- 2 tablespoons tomato sauce (ketchup)
- 2 eggs, beaten
- milk to mix

MUSHROOM SAUCE

- 40 g (1⅓ oz) butter
- 2 tablespoons plain (all-purpose) flour
- 1 cup (250 ml/8 fl oz) chicken stock
- 30 g (1 oz) sliced button mushrooms
- freshly ground black pepper

Preheat oven to 160°C (325°F).

Use food processor to mince crumbs and chop ingredients. Combine all loaf ingredients, adding enough milk to ensure that mixture is not too dry. Pour into greased loaf pan, and bake for 1 hour or until cooked.

To make sauce: Melt butter in a saucepan, stir in flour and cook 1 minute, stirring continuously. Add stock and bring to the boil stirring constantly. Add mushrooms and cook a further 3 minutes. Season to taste with black pepper. Alternatively, the sauce can be made in the microwave oven.

Serve Chicken Loaf in thick slices with mushroom sauce, creamy mashed potatoes and peas or beans.

SERVES 6

TURKISH CHICKEN WITH VEGETABLES

- 500 g (1 lb) eggplant (aubergine), peeled and sliced
- salt
- 1 x 1.5 kg (3 lb) chicken, cut into serving pieces or 1 kg (2 lb) chicken pieces
- 3 tablespoons seasoned flour
- ¼ cup (60 ml/2 fl oz) olive oil
- 2 onions, thinly sliced
- 1 green capsicum (pepper), seeded and cut into strips
- 2 small zucchini (courgettes), thinly sliced
- 4 ripe tomatoes, peeled and sliced
- 250 g (8 oz) fresh or drained canned okra
- 250 g (8 oz) green beans, halved
- 1½ cups (375 ml/12 fl oz) chicken stock

Preheat oven to 180°C (350°F).

Sprinkle the eggplant with salt and set aside for 15 minutes. Rinse eggplant slices and pat dry on paper towels.

Toss chicken pieces in seasoned flour. Fry the chicken in the hot oil for 10 to 15 minutes, until golden brown. Remove from pan and keep warm.

Add the onions, capsicum and eggplant and fry for 3 minutes. Add zucchini, tomatoes, okra and beans and fry 1 minute longer.

Transfer all the vegetables to a casserole. Place the chicken pieces on top of the vegetables. Add chicken stock, cover and cook for 40 to 45 minutes or until cooked.

Serve from the casserole accompanied by brown rice or warm Turkish bread.

SERVES 4

ROAST MOROCCAN CHICKEN

- 1 x 1.5 kg (3 lb) dressed chicken
- 1 onion, chopped
- ½ teaspoon salt
- 1¼ cups (300 ml/10 fl oz) natural yoghurt
- 375 g (12 oz) cooked rice (155 g (5 oz) raw)
- 125 g (4 oz) cooked or frozen peas
- 60 g (2 oz) pine nuts
- salt and pepper
- juice of 1 large orange

Place chicken in a non-metallic dish. Add onion and salt to yoghurt, spoon over chicken, cover and marinate in refrigerator for several hours.

Preheat oven to 180°C (350°F).

Combine remaining ingredients (except orange juice) season to taste with salt and pepper and stuff chicken with mixture. Truss. Place in a roasting pan, add orange juice. Bake for 1 to 1¼ hours or until tender, basting occasionally.

Serve chicken with stuffing, glazed carrots and fried mushrooms.

SERVES 4

CHICKEN ANDALUSIA

12 pieces chicken (on the bone)

3 tablespoons seasoned flour

2 tablespoons olive oil

60 g (2 oz) butter

1 large onion, chopped

1 clove garlic, crushed

1 green capsicum (pepper), seeded and chopped

100 g (3⅓ oz) button mushrooms, chopped

2 tomatoes, thickly sliced

12 g (⅓ oz) chopped fresh parsley

¾ cup (180 ml/6 fl oz) chicken stock

¼ cup (60 ml/2 fl oz) white wine

90 g (3 oz) black olives

½ cup (125 ml/4 fl oz) cream

Preheat oven to 180°C (350°F).

Trim excess fat from chicken and coat with seasoned flour. Heat oil and butter in a large frying pan, add chicken and cook until golden. Transfer to a shallow casserole. Cook onion and garlic in the pan until soft. Add capsicum and mushrooms and cook for 2 minutes. Spoon vegetables over chicken and add tomato. Sprinkle with parsley. Pour over stock and wine and cook, uncovered, in oven for 45 minutes or until tender. Add olives and cream during last 10 minutes.

Serve hot accompanied by rice and green salad.

SERVES 6

CHICKEN AND MUSHROOM PIE

2 chicken breast fillets, skinned

4 chicken thigh fillets

2 tablespoons oil

375 g (12 oz) button mushrooms

125 g (4 oz) small pickling onions, peeled

2 tablespoons plain (all-purpose) flour

2 tomatoes, peeled and chopped

¾ cup (180 ml/6 fl oz) dry white wine

½ cup (125 ml/4 fl oz) chicken stock

salt and pepper

2 sheets pre-rolled puff pastry

egg for glazing

Cut chicken into bite-sized pieces. Heat oil in a pan and brown chicken pieces for 10 minutes. Add mushrooms and onions and stir until lightly browned. Sprinkle in flour and stir for 1 minute. Stir in tomatoes, wine and stock and season to taste with salt and pepper. Bring to the boil, cover and simmer 30 minutes. Allow to cool.

Preheat oven to 200°C (400°F).

Roll out one sheet of pastry on a lightly floured board to 5 mm (¼ in) thickness and line a 20 cm (8 in) pie plate. Fill pie with chicken and mushroom filling. Roll out second sheet of pastry to 5 mm (¼ in) thick. Cover pie, trim off excess pastry and seal edges with a little cold water. Flake and flute edge of pie. Decorate with leaves of pastry and brush with beaten egg. Bake for 30 to 40 minutes until pastry is golden brown and cooked.

Serve pie with carrots and Brussels sprouts or beans.

SERVES 6

Spatchcock with Prunes, Cumquats and Almonds is pictured on the front cover.

SPATCHCOCK WITH PRUNES, CUMQUATS AND ALMONDS

6 spatchcock, each about 400 g to 500 g (13 oz to 16 oz)

125 g (4 oz) butter

1 teaspoon ground cumin

1 clove garlic, peeled and finely chopped

salt and freshly ground black pepper

SAUCE

90 g (3 oz) butter

150 g (5 oz) blanched almonds

180 g (6 oz) pitted prunes

1½ cups (375 ml/12½ fl oz) chicken stock

90 g (3 oz) black olives

4 small red chillies, seeded and sliced

200 g (6½ oz) cumquats, halved

125 g (4 oz) preserved lemons, sliced (available from good delicatessens)

Preheat oven to 170°C (325°F).

Wash spatchcock and pat dry. Tie legs together with string. Melt the butter with cumin and garlic. Brush all over spatchcock and place birds in a roasting dish. Sprinkle with salt and freshly ground black pepper. Roast for 1½ hours, brushing frequently with butter. Place birds under grill for 5 minutes to finish browning.

To prepare sauce: Melt butter in a saucepan, add almonds and fry over a moderate heat until golden. Add remaining ingredients and simmer for 10 minutes. Pour pan juices from birds into sauce and simmer for 5 minutes. Serve birds with sauce spooned over, accompanied by cous cous and watercress.

Note: Instant cous cous is available from supermarkets and delicatessens.

SERVES 6

MUSTARD ROAST CHICKEN

1.5 kg (3 lb) dressed chicken

juice of 1 lemon

1 x 120 g (approximately 4 oz) jar French mustard

40 g (1⅓ oz) butter

1 cup (250 ml/8 fl oz) white wine

1 cup (250 ml/8 fl oz) cream

2 egg yolks

Preheat oven to 180°C (350°F).

Sprinkle chicken with lemon juice. Reserve 1½ tablespoons mustard for sauce and mix remaining mustard with butter and spread over chicken. Roast for 1 hour or until tender, turning bird every 15 minutes and basting each time with mustard mixture. Remove chicken and keep warm.

Boil wine in a saucepan until reduced by half. Mix reserved mustard with cream and egg yolks. Allow the wine to cool slightly and slowly pour in the cream mixture, stirring. Stir in juices from roasting pan and warm through.

Serve roast chicken with mustard sauce, roast potatoes and freshly cooked vegetables.

SERVES 4

Mustard Roast Chicken

STUFFED CAPSICUMS (PEPPERS)

6 large green capsicums (pepper)

75 g (2½ oz) long grain rice

3 tablespoons olive oil

1 onion, chopped

2 cloves garlic, crushed

2 tablespoons pine nuts

500 g (1 lb) chicken mince

40 g (1½ oz) raisins

2 tablespoons honey

1 teaspoon salt

freshly ground black pepper

1 teaspoon chopped fresh thyme or ¼ teaspoon dried thyme

pinch of ground ginger

1½ cups (375 ml/12 fl oz) tomato juice

Preheat oven to 190°C (375°F).

Cut a slice from the top of each capsicum. If they don't stand upright, cut a thin slice from the base. Remove all seeds and white membrane. Blanch in boiling water for 2 to 3 minutes. Drain thoroughly. Cook rice in boiling water to cover for 10 minutes; drain immediately.

Heat half the oil in a frying pan, add onion, garlic and pine nuts and cook for 3 to 4 minutes. Add chicken and cook, stirring over a low heat for 5 minutes until browned. Mix in rice, raisins, honey, salt, pepper, thyme, ginger and ⅔ cup (160 ml/5 fl oz) tomato juice.

Brush outsides of capsicums lightly with oil. Stuff capsicums with chicken mixture and arrange in shallow casserole. Stand them upright. Sprinkle 1 tablespoon oil over capsicums. Pour remaining tomato juice and oil around capsicums and bake for 45 minutes. Spoon sauce over before serving.

Serve with brown rice and salad.

SERVES 6

Cut slice from top of each capsicum. Remove seeds and membrane.

Cook filling ingredients over low heat.

Stuff capsicums with filling mixture. Arrange in shallow casserole and pour over remaining tomato juice and oil.

CITRUS BAKED CHICKEN

1½ kg (3 lb) chicken pieces

3 tablespoons seasoned flour

30 g (1 oz) butter or margarine

2 tablespoons oil

1 onion, thickly sliced

1½ tablespoons plain (all-purpose) flour

2 cups (500 ml/16 fl oz) chicken stock

½ cup (125 ml/4 fl oz) dry white wine

juice and thinly sliced rind of 1 orange

1 tablespoon Worcestershire sauce

60 g (2 oz) sultanas

seasonings, to taste

Preheat oven to 180°C (350°F).

Dust chicken in seasoned flour, shaking off excess. Heat butter and oil in a large frying pan. Brown chicken well on all sides. Transfer to a casserole dish.

Sauté onion in same pan until tender. Place in casserole.

Sprinkle flour into pan. Cook, stirring, for 1 minute. Remove from heat. Gradually blend in combined stock, wine, orange juice and Worcestershire sauce.

Return to heat. Cook, stirring constantly, until sauce boils and thickens. Simmer for 3 minutes. Stir in sultanas, orange rind and seasonings.

Pour sauce over chicken. Bake for about 1 hour or until chicken is cooked and tender. Serve with rice and salad.

SERVES 4 TO 6

RIVERLAND CHICKEN

8 chicken drumsticks or 4 portions chicken Maryland

¾ cup (180 ml/6 fl oz) orange juice

grated rind of 1 orange

¼ cup (60 ml/2 fl oz) water

1 tablespoon grated onion

125 g (4 oz) butter, melted

1 tablespoon chopped fresh parsley or 1 teaspoon dried mixed herbs

125 g (4 oz) dry breadcrumbs

2 teaspoons cornflour (cornstarch)

2 tablespoons water

1 tablespoon sweet chilli sauce

cooked noodles or rice to serve

Trim chicken joints neatly. Combine orange juice, orange rind, water and onion. Marinate chicken in orange mixture, covered in refrigerator, overnight turning once. Drain chicken and reserve the marinade.

Preheat oven to 180°C (350°F).

Mix butter with herbs and brush generously over chicken. Sprinkle with crumbs and press firmly into buttered coating. Line a shallow ovenproof dish with foil and place chicken pieces in it in a single layer. Sprinkle with any leftover butter. Cover lightly with foil and bake for 30 minutes. Remove foil cover. Turn chicken and bake uncovered for 20 to 30 minutes until tender.

To make the sauce, blend cornflour with 2 tablespoons water. Add to marinade in a saucepan with chilli sauce. Cook, stirring, until thickened. Add any liquid remaining from cooked chicken.

Alternatively, the sauce can be microwaved in a glass jug for 1 minute, stirred and then cooked a further 30 seconds until sauce has thickened.

Serve chicken with orange sauce, pasta noodles or multigrain rice and zucchini (courgettes) or sugar snap peas.

SERVES 4

SEGMENTING CHICKEN

Segment a chicken into 8 serving pieces by removing leg and thigh at joint and halving through thigh joint; removing wing and part of breast and then chopping breast from carcass and halving through the breast bone. If you prefer, purchase pieces.

COQ AU VIN

This recipe uses speck, which is a beautifully flavoured cured pork. It is particularly popular in Europe and is used here to add texture and a smoky flavour to this traditional French dish. If speck is not available, substitute shoulder bacon.

12 chicken pieces (on the bone)

1½ cups (375 ml/12 fl oz) red wine

1 onion, chopped

1 carrot, chopped

½ teaspoon dried thyme

2 bay leaves

2 sprigs parsley

2 teaspoons salt

1 knob garlic, crushed (not just a clove)

30 g (1 oz) plain (all-purpose) flour

2 tablespoons olive oil

80 g (2⅔ oz) butter

125 g (4 oz) smoked speck, chopped

extra 1 onion, chopped

extra 30 g (1 oz) butter

4 black olives, chopped

Trim chicken pieces of excess fat and skin. Mix wine, onion, carrot, herbs, salt and garlic together and marinate chicken in mixture for 2 hours, turning occasionally.

Drain chicken, reserving marinade. Roll chicken in flour and cook gently in oil and half the butter until browned. Add marinade and cook over low heat or bake at 180°C (350°F) for 45 minutes until tender. Mix remaining butter with 2 tablespoons extra flour and drop in a little at a time, stirring thoroughly, until thickened.

Fry speck with extra onion in 30 g butter. Add to chicken with black olives and continue to cook for 10 to 15 minutes until heated through.

Serve hot with rice and a tossed salad.

SERVES 6

CARIBBEAN CHICKEN AND RICE

8 pieces chicken (on the bone)

1 tablespoon chopped fresh oregano or 1 teaspoon dried oregano

1 teaspoon salt

freshly ground black pepper

1 tablespoon fresh lime or lemon juice

250 g (8 oz) bacon, chopped

2 tablespoons oil

1 green capsicum (pepper), seeded and chopped

1 red capsicum (pepper), seeded and chopped

1 onion, chopped

2 cloves garlic, crushed

250 g (8 oz) cooked ham, sliced

1 tomato, peeled and chopped

12 stuffed olives

1 tablespoon capers

220 g (7 oz) long grain rice

2½ cups (625 ml/20 fl oz) chicken stock

300 g (10 oz) frozen peas, thawed

Trim excess fat and skin from chicken. Rub chicken with oregano, salt, pepper and lime juice and leave to marinate for 1 hour.

Fry bacon in a large heavy-based pan until crisp. Add oil, capsicums, onion, garlic and ham and fry gently for 10 minutes. Add chicken and fry gently until brown. Stir in tomato, olives, capers and rice and cook, stirring, for a few minutes. Add stock, cover and cook for 35 to 45 minutes until chicken is tender. Stir in peas and cook for 5 minutes until peas are tender.

Serve hot with garlic bread and a green salad.

SERVES 4

Barbecue Chicken

*C*hicken cooked on a barbecue is very popular. It is quick to cook, free of fat and gristle, easy to eat and lends itself to marinating with fragrant or flavoursome ingredients.

CHICKEN TIKKA KEBABS

Tikka curry is a specialty of the Punjab. Tikka paste is available in leading Asian stores.

250 g (8 oz) chicken thigh fillets, skinned

250 g (8 oz) chicken breast fillets, skinned

4 tablespoons tikka paste

½ cup (125 ml/4 fl oz) natural yoghurt

mango chutney and lettuce leaves to serve

Trim chicken and cut into 2 cm (¾ in) cubes or pieces. Mix tikka paste with yoghurt, pour over chicken and marinate, covered, in the refrigerator overnight. Thread onto pre-soaked bamboo skewers and cook on a barbecue hotplate for 10 minutes, turning frequently and brushing with any leftover marinade, until cooked.

Serve each kebab topped with chutney and wrapped up in a lettuce leaf as a first course at a barbecue party.

SERVES 8

BAMBOO SKEWERS

Soak bamboo skewers in water before use. This will prevent them burning.

HONEY AND SOY KEBABS

Young children love the sweet-spicy flavour of these kebabs

4 chicken breast fillets, skinned

16 button mushrooms

chopped fresh parsley or mint to sprinkle

MARINADE

2 tablespoons light soy sauce

2 tablespoons honey

1 tablespoon white vinegar

1 tablespoon cornflour (cornstarch)

2 tablespoons tomato sauce

1 clove garlic, crushed, optional

Trim chicken and cut into 2½ cm (1 in) cubes. Trim mushroom stalks and wipe clean.

Marinade: Mix all ingredients together. Add chicken to marinade and mix until well coated. Cover and marinate in refrigerator for at least 2 hours.

Thread chicken onto 8 pre-soaked bamboo skewers with 2 button mushrooms per skewer. Cook on a barbecue hot plate over a medium–hot barbecue, brushing with marinade and turning frequently until cooked, about 10 minutes. Sprinkle with chopped herbs.

Serve Honey and Soy Kebabs with rice and salad.

SERVES 4 TO 8

SPICY INDONESIAN KEBABS

Popular with adults who like spicy hot food

250 g (8 oz) chicken thigh fillets, skinned

250 g (8 oz) chicken breast fillets, skinned

juice of 1 lime

1 teaspoon salt

10 French shallots or 1 large onion, peeled

4 cloves garlic, peeled and halved

4 red chillies, seeded

2½ cm (1 in) slice ginger, peeled

2 teaspoons shrimp paste

2 tablespoons oil

2 tomatoes, seeded and chopped

Cut chicken into 2½ cm (1 in) pieces, mix with lime juice and salt. Place all remaining ingredients except tomatoes in a food processor or blender and mix to a paste. Place paste in a pan and bring to the boil. Add tomatoes and cook for 1 minute, stirring continuously. Pour over chicken and mix well, cover and marinate in refrigerator for at least 1 hour.

Thread chicken onto 8 pre-soaked bamboo skewers, mixing chicken thigh meat with breast meat. Cook on the hotplate over a medium–high barbecue, turning and brushing frequently with remaining marinade until tender, about 10 minutes.

Serve kebabs hot with rice salad and green salad.

SERVES 4 TO 8

Dishes on previous pages: Honey and Soy Kebabs (page 84), Barbecued Balinese Poussin (page 90)

CHICKEN LIVER KEBABS

6 rashers thinly sliced bacon, rind removed

1 firm tomato

12 chicken livers

2 chicken breast fillets, skinned and cubed

½ green capsicum (pepper), cubed

½ red capsicum (pepper), cubed

12 pickling onions, peeled

6 button mushrooms, halved

6 fresh bay leaves

salt and pepper

juice of 1 lemon

2 tablespoons olive oil

Cut each bacon rasher in half. Cut tomato into 6 or 12 wedges depending on size. Clean chicken livers, cut into lobes and wrap each lobe in a piece of bacon.

Thread prepared ingredients and bay leaves alternately onto 6 long, pre-soaked skewers. Season kebabs with salt and pepper and brush with lemon juice and oil. Cook under medium grill or on a barbecue.

Serve kebabs with boiled rice and salad.

SERVES 6

PICKLING ONIONS

Pickling onions are baby onions often available at your greengrocer. If unavailable use small onions or halve or quarter larger ones.

YAKITORI

3 chicken breast fillets, skinned

8 spring onions (shallots)

3 tablespoons mirin, sake (Japanese wine) or dry sherry

2 tablespoons soy sauce

2 teaspoons ginger root, finely shredded

1 clove garlic, crushed

Cut each chicken breast into 2 cm (¾ in) cubes. Cut white of spring onions into 2½ cm (1 in) lengths. Thread onto satay sticks, alternating chicken cubes with spring onion pieces.

Blend mirin, soy sauce, ginger and garlic and brush over chicken, allowing it to marinate for 15 minutes.

Yakitori can be grilled or barbecued or cooked in a lightly oiled pan. Cooking time is about 8 to 10 minutes. Turn and baste during cooking to ensure even browning.

Serve as a finger-licking first course at a barbecue party.

SERVES 6

CRUSHED GARLIC

Crush garlic cloves by chopping finely and then pressing with the blade of a knife to crush. A little salt sprinkled onto the clove before crushing will absorb any garlic juice that escapes. Alternatively, use a garlic press.

TERIYAKI CHICKEN DRUMSTICKS

1 onion, chopped

2 cloves garlic, crushed

½ cup (125 ml/4 fl oz) soy sauce

1 cup (250 ml/8 fl oz) water

2 tablespoons brown sugar

1 teaspoon chopped ginger

1 kg (2 lb) chicken drumsticks

toasted sesame seeds to garnish

Combine onion and garlic with soy sauce, water, brown sugar and ginger. Pour over chicken and marinate covered in a refrigerator for 12 hours. Barbecue or grill over medium heat for 25 minutes until tender, turning frequently and brushing with remaining marinade.

Sprinkle with sesame seeds to serve and accompany with a rice salad.

SERVES 4

LOW FAT CHICKEN

Remove skin from chicken pieces to reduce fat, cholesterol and kilojoules. Skin is easily removed from chicken pieces. Simply ease fingertips under skin and pull.

LEMON CHICKEN WINGS

1 kg (2 lb) chicken wings

MARINADE

4 tablespoons tomato sauce

4 tablespoons fresh lemon juice

4 tablespoons soy sauce

1/2 teaspoon ground ginger

Combine marinade ingredients and mix with wings to cover. Refrigerate for 3 to 4 hours or overnight. Barbecue for 10 to 15 minutes, turning and basting frequently.

Serve for a finger-licking barbecue party first course.

SERVES 8 TO 10

BARBECUE BASTED CHICKEN

12 chicken pieces (on the bone)

BARBECUE SAUCE

3 cloves garlic, crushed

1½ cups (375 ml/12 fl oz) tomato juice

¾ cup (180 ml/6 fl oz) cider vinegar

3 tablespoons oil

1 tablespoon Worcestershire sauce

1 teaspoon sugar

¼ teaspoon pepper

¼ teaspoon cayenne

¼ teaspoon mustard powder

Trim excess fat and skin from chicken pieces.

Lemon Chicken Wings

Combine Barbecue Sauce ingredients in a saucepan. Bring to the boil and simmer 10 minutes.

Arrange chicken pieces evenly on a baking tray. Brush with sauce. Bake for 1¼ hours at 180°C (350°F) or barbecue over a medium heat, turning and brushing frequently with Barbecue Sauce until the chicken is cooked and tender (about 30 to 40 minutes).

Serve with jacket baked potatoes topped with sour cream or potato salad and coleslaw.

SERVES 6

Barbecue Basted Chicken

BARBECUED CHICKEN BURGERS

Popular with children and easy to prepare, store, transport and eat!

1 small onion, finely chopped

1 teaspoon olive oil

500 g (1 lb) chicken mince

2 tablespoons chopped parsley or basil

¼ teaspoon salt

freshly ground black pepper

8 hamburger buns

8 mignonette lettuce leaves

8 large slices tomato

thinly sliced cucumber

tartare sauce, optional

Gently fry onion in oil until soft. Mix fried onion with chicken mince, herb, salt and pepper. Divide into eight equal portions and shape into round patties or burgers. Cook burgers on an oiled barbecue hotplate over a medium–high heat, turning carefully, until golden and cooked in the centre.

Serve Chicken Burgers in split hamburger buns on layered lettuce, tomato and cucumber and top with tartare sauce if liked.

SERVES 8

CRANBERRY DRUMSTICKS

1 x 250 g (8 oz) jar cranberry sauce

¼ cup (60 ml/2 fl oz) soy sauce

½ teaspoon crushed garlic

2 tablespoons fresh lemon juice

12 chicken drumsticks, trimmed

salt and pepper

12 rashers bacon

Combine sauces, garlic and lemon juice. Bring to the boil and simmer for 5 minutes until smooth.

Sprinkle chicken with salt and pepper. Remove rind and bones from bacon. Wrap each drumstick in a rasher of bacon, fastening ends with toothpicks. Cook slowly on a barbecue over a medium heat, turning and brushing frequently with the sauce.

Serve hot with barbecued corn on the cob, jacket baked potatoes and salad.

SERVES 6

BARBECUE HINTS

Remember to scrape your barbecue plate between courses so that the flavours of the individual dishes are preserved.

COOKING

It is important to ensure that your barbecued chicken is well cooked so make sure the pieces are flattened and evenly thick.

SPICY THAI BARBECUED CHICKEN

1.5 kg (3 lb) chicken pieces, breasts and thighs (on the bone)

1 teaspoon salt

freshly ground black pepper

125 g (4 oz) butter

juice of 4 limes

2 cloves garlic, crushed

2 teaspoons brown sugar

2 teaspoons chopped ginger

1 teaspoon chopped chilli

2 tablespoons sliced lemon grass

1 tablespoon chopped coriander (cilantro) root

2 tablespoons chopped coriander (cilantro) leaves

Sprinkle chicken with salt and pepper.

Melt butter in a saucepan and add remaining ingredients. Stir well.

Brush chickens with spicy mixture and place on an oiled rack, skin side up, over a hot charcoal fire. Grill for 15 to 20 minutes on each side, basting frequently with sauce.

Serve with hot cooked rice or a spicy rice salad and cucumber salad.

SERVES 8

CHICKEN TANDOORI

- 1 x 1.5 kg (3 lb) chicken, quartered
- 1 x 200 g (approximately 6 oz) carton natural yoghurt
- 1 tablespoon paprika
- 1 tablespoon tomato paste (purée)
- ½ teaspoon salt
- ½ teaspoon ground ginger
- ½ teaspoon crushed garlic
- 6 peppercorns, cracked
- 4 bay leaves
- grated zest of 1 lemon
- lemon wedges and coriander (cilantro) to garnish

Remove backbone, wing tips and excess fat from chicken quarters.

Skin chicken and prick flesh well with a fork or skewer. Mix all remaining ingredients together for marinade. Add chicken, making sure all pieces are completely covered. Cover tightly and leave 6 hours or overnight in the refrigerator. Remove bay leaves.

Arrange chicken on a wire rack in a roasting pan. Brush each piece with marinade. Bake at 180°C (350°F) for 1¼ hours or until chicken is tender, basting every 15 minutes.

Alternatively cook on a hotplate over a barbecue fire, turning and brushing frequently with marinade for 30 to 40 minutes or until tender.

Serve Chicken Tandoori garnished with lemon wedges and coriander, accompanied by curry sambals and hot cooked rice.

SERVES 4

SAMBALS

These are side dishes which make good accompaniments for curries and vindaloos. Try some of these ideas:

- Mix low fat natural yoghurt with chopped cucumber and fresh mint.

- Combine sliced bananas with chopped chilli and lemon juice, or use apple instead of banana.

- Mix 1 cup coconut milk with chopped onion, crushed garlic and chilli powder.

- Make up your own selection of vegetables, blanch them and combine with chopped chillies, lemon juice, a little oil and desiccated coconut.

GOLDEN CHICKEN

- 6 chicken Maryland thighs
- 2 tablespoons curry powder or paste
- ½ cup (125 ml/4 fl oz) honey
- 3 tablespoons orange or pineapple juice
- 2 cloves garlic, crushed
- 2 tablespoons French wholegrain mustard
- ½ teaspoon ground cardamom

Drop chicken into boiling water and simmer slowly for 10 minutes. Drain and dry. Sprinkle curry powder over chicken or spread paste over. Warm honey with juice, garlic, mustard and cardamom until honey dissolves.

Paint over chicken and barbecue over a medium heat for 20 to 25 minutes until tender, basting and turning frequently.

Serve with barbecued bananas and pineapple rings and accompany with a rice salad and a green salad.

SERVES 6

SERVIETTES

Remember to provide your guests with plenty of good quality serviettes while eating these barbecued treats.

LEMON HERB BARBECUE CHICKEN

- 1 x 1.5 kg (3 lb) chicken, quartered

MARINADE

- 1 cup (250 ml/8 fl oz) olive oil
- ½ cup (125 ml/4 fl oz) fresh lemon juice
- ½ teaspoon salt
- 2 tablespoons shredded fresh basil or mint
- 2 tablespoons chopped fresh parsley
- 2 tablespoons snipped fresh chives
- 1 teaspoon paprika

Remove backbone, excess skin and fat from chicken quarters. Place in a shallow dish in a single layer.

Combine marinade ingredients. Pour over chicken and marinate overnight or for 6 hours. Barbecue over medium heat for 25 to 35 minutes until tender.

Serve Lemon Herb Barbecue Chicken with pasta salad and cherry tomato salad.

SERVES 4

BARBECUED BALINESE POUSSIN

Use a food processor or blender to save time when chopping the ingredients for this dish.

  2 large poussin or spatchcock

  juice of 1 lemon or 2 limes

  ½ teaspoon salt

  2 tablespoons peanut or safflower oil

  8 French shallots, finely chopped

  2 cloves garlic, crushed

  1 tablespoon finely chopped ginger

  2 green chillies, seeded and chopped

  1 stalk lemon grass, thinly sliced

  3 tablespoons shredded mint

  3 tablespoons shredded basil

  2 vine ripened tomatoes, finely chopped

Cut the poussin in half lengthwise leave skin intact but remove and discard backbone. Score each halved poussin diagonally. Sprinkle with lemon juice and salt. Heat oil and gently fry shallots, garlic, ginger, chillies and lemon grass until soft. Remove from heat and stir in herbs and tomatoes. Spread over the poussin and marinate for at least 1 hour. Cook over a medium–hot barbecue for 30 to 40 minutes, turning and brushing with the marinade frequently, until cooked.

Serve barbecued poussin with a rice salad and a green salad.

SERVES 4

Barbecued Balinese Poussin

CHICKEN
MACADAMIA KEBABS

4 chicken breast fillets, skinned

1 Spanish (red) onion

1 red capsicum (pepper)

2 cups broccoli florets

MARINADE

1 onion, finely chopped

1 clove garlic, crushed

3 tablespoons fresh lemon juice

3 tablespoons light soy sauce

2 tablespoons macadamia nut oil

2 tablespoons ground macadamia nuts

1 teaspoon ground coriander (cilantro)

1 teaspoon tabasco sauce

freshly ground black pepper

Cut chicken into 3 cm (1¼ in) cubes.

To make marinade: Combine marinade ingredients in a bowl. Add chicken to marinade and stir until evenly coated. Cover and marinate in refrigerator for 3 to 4 hours.

Chicken Macadamia Kebabs

Cut onion into wedges then cut each wedge in half. Cut pepper into 2 cm (¾ in) squares. Prepare broccoli.

Thread chicken and vegetables alternately onto pre-soaked bamboo skewers. Barbecue over a medium heat for 15 to 20 minutes or until cooked, turning and brushing frequently with the remaining marinade.

Serve kebabs with spicy lemon rice.

SERVES 4

MEASURING MADE EASY

HOW TO MEASURE DRY INGREDIENTS

15 g	½ oz	
30 g	1 oz	
60 g	2 oz	
90 g	3 oz	
125 g	4 oz	(¼ lb)
155 g	5 oz	
185 g	6 oz	
220 g	7 oz	
250 g	8 oz	(½ lb)
280 g	9 oz	
315 g	10 oz	
345 g	11 oz	
375 g	12 oz	(¾ lb)
410 g	13 oz	
440 g	14 oz	
470 g	15 oz	
500 g	16 oz	(1 lb)
750 g	24 oz	(1½ lb)
1 kg	32 oz	(2 lb)

QUICK CONVERSIONS

5 mm	¼ inch	
1 cm	½ inch	
2 cm	¾ inch	
2.5 cm	1 inch	
5 cm	2 inches	
6 cm	2½ inches	
8 cm	3 inches	
10 cm	4 inches	
12 cm	5 inches	
15 cm	6 inches	
18 cm	7 inches	
20 cm	8 inches	
23 cm	9 inches	
25 cm	10 inches	
28 cm	11 inches	
30 cm	12 inches	(1 foot)
46 cm	18 inches	
50 cm	20 inches	
61 cm	24 inches	(2 feet)
77 cm	30 inches	

NOTE: We developed the recipes in this book in Australia where the tablespoon measure is 20 ml. In many other countries the tablespoon is 15 ml. For most recipes this difference will not be noticeable.

However, for recipes using baking powder, gelatine, bicarbonate of soda, small amounts of flour and cornflour, we suggest you add an extra teaspoon for each tablespoon specified.

Many people find it very convenient to use cup measurements. You can buy special measuring cups or measure water in an ordinary household cup to check it holds 250 ml (8 fl oz). This can then be used for both liquid and dry cup measurements.

MEASURING LIQUIDS

METRIC CUPS

¼ cup	60 ml	2 fluid ounces
⅓ cup	80 ml	2½ fluid ounces
½ cup	125 ml	4 fluid ounces
¾ cup	180 ml	6 fluid ounces
1 cup	250 ml	8 fluid ounces

METRIC SPOONS

¼ teaspoon	1.25 ml
½ teaspoon	2.5 ml
1 teaspoon	5 ml
1 tablespoon	20 ml

OVEN TEMPERATURES

TEMPERATURES	CELSIUS (°C)	FAHRENHEIT (°F)	GAS MARK
Very Slow	120	250	½
Slow	150	300	2
Moderate	160–180	325–350	3–4
Moderately hot	190–200	375–400	5–6
Hot	220–230	425–450	7–8
Very hot	250–260	475–500	9–10

Published by Murdoch Books®,
a division of Murdoch Magazines Pty Ltd,
213 Miller Street, North Sydney NSW 2060.

Front Cover Photography: Jon Bader.
Chapter Opening Photography: Quentin Bacon.
Food Editor: Anne Marshall.
Front Cover Food Stylist: Carolyn Fienberg.
Chapter Opener Food Stylist: Anne Marshall.
Food Stylist's Assistant: Ann Bollard.
Jacket design: Sylvie Abecassis.
Front cover recipe: Tuscan Chicken (page 73).
Back cover recipe: Chicken Mole (page 65).

Managing Editor: Jane Price.
Food Editors: Kerrie Ray, Tracy Rutherford.
Publisher: Anne Wilson.
International Sales Manager: Mark Newman.

National Library of Australia Cataloguing-in-Publication Data:
All occasion chicken cookbook. New ed. Includes index.
ISBN 0 86411 574 1. 1. Cookery (Chicken). I. Marshall, Anne, 1938-.
(Series: Bay Books cookery collection). 641.665.
First published in Australia in 1994. This edition first printed 1996.
Printed by Griffin Press, Adelaide.

Glossary of Terms

AUSTRALIAN	UK	USA
EQUIPMENT AND TERMS		
aluminium foil	cooking foil	aluminum foil
can	tin	can
frying pan	frying pan	skillet
griller	grill	broiler
greaseproof paper	greaseproof paper	waxproof paper
paper towel	kitchen paper	white paper towel
plastic wrap	cling film	plastic wrap
seeded	stoned	pitted
INGREDIENTS		
artichoke	globe artichoke	artichoke
bacon rasher	bacon rasher	bacon slice
black olive	black olive	ripe olive
broad bean	broad bean	fava bean
butternut pumpkin		butternut squash
capsicum	pepper	sweet pepper
chicken breast fillets	chicken breast fillets	boneless chicken breasts
chickpea	chickpea	garbanzo bean
chilli	chilli	chili
coriander (fresh)	coriander/Indian parsley	cilantro/Chinese parsley
corn kernels	sweet corn	corn kernels
cornflour	cornflour	cornstarch
cornmeal	polenta/maize meal	cornmeal
cream	single cream	light cream
desiccated coconut	desiccated coconut	shredded coconut
dill	dill	dill weed
eggplant	aubergine	eggplant
gelatine	gelatine powder	gelatin
pawpaw	pawpaw	papaya or papaw
pine nut	pine nut	pignolias
plain flour	(general purpose) flour	all-purpose flour
prawn	prawn or shrimp	shrimp
shallots	spring onions	scallions/green onions
silver beet (spinach)	silver beet (chard)	Swiss chard
snow pea	mangetout, sugar pea	snow pea
soybean	soyabean	soybean
sultanas	sultanas	seedless white or golden raisins
thickened cream	double cream	heavy or whipping cream
tomato paste	tomato purée	tomato paste
Worcestershire sauce	Worcester sauce	Worchestershire sauce
yoghurt	natural yogurt	unflavoured yoghurt
zucchini	courgette	zucchini